Good News About
Sex and Marriage

Good News About Sex and Marriage

Answers to Your Honest Questions
About Catholic Teaching

CHRISTOPHER WEST

CHARIS

SERVANT PUBLICATIONS
ANN ARBOR, MICHIGAN

Charis Books is an imprint of Servant Publications designed to serve Roman Catholics.

All Scripture quotations, unless otherwise indicated, are taken from the Revised Standard Version of the Bible, copyrighted 1946, 1952, 1971 by the Division of Christian Education of the National Council of Churches of Christ in the USA. Used by permission.

Excerpts from the English translation of the *Catechism of the Catholic Church* for use in the United States of America. Copyright © 1994, United States Catholic Conference, Inc.-Libreria Editrice Vaticana. Used with permission.

Excerpts from the English translation of the *Catechism of the Catholic Church: Modifications from the "Editio Typica"*. Copyright © 1997, United States Catholic Conference, Inc.-Libreria Editrice Vaticana. Used with Permission.

Published by Servant Publications
P.O. Box 8617
Ann Arbor, Michigan 48107

Nihil obstat: Reverend Gerard Beigel, S.T.D.
                  Censor Librorum
Imprimatur: Most Reverend Charles J. Chaput, O.F.M. Cap.
                  Archbishop of Denver
July 28, 2000
The *nihil obstat* and *imprimatur* are official declarations that a book is free from doctrinal or moral error. No implication is contained therein that those who grant the *nihil obstat* or *imprimatur* agree with the contents, opinions, or statements expressed.

        02   03   10   9

Printed in the United States of America
ISBN 0-56955-214-2

LIBRARY OF CONGRESS CATALOGING-IN-PUBLICATION DATA

West, Christopher, 1969-
    Good news about sex and marriage : answers to your honest questions about Catholic teaching / Christopher West.
        p.   cm.
    Includes bibliographical references.
    ISBN 1-56955-214-2 (alk. paper)
    1. Sex—Religious aspects—Catholic Church.   2. Marriage—Religious aspects—Catholic Church.   3. Catholic Church—Doctrines.   I. Title.

BX1795.S48 W47 2000
241'.66—dc21   00-043182

To my beloved bride, Wendy.
Without her love of my manhood I would not be who I am,
nor could I have written this book.

Contents

Foreword

Here's a safe bet: I'd wager that most of you who open this book have heard about a "vocation crisis" in the Church. Over the past thirty years, it's been a popular topic of conversation. Thousands of articles have been written about it. You've probably seen your share.

Here's another safe bet: I'd wager that nearly all those stories and conversations dealt with priests or religious—how few we have, and why we'll have even fewer in the future. And of course, we do need more priests and religious, and in many areas of the United States, the decline in their numbers is extremely serious.

But here's a third safe bet: I'd wager that very few of those articles and conversations dealt with the most fundamental vocations crisis of all: marriage and family life. God calls every one of us by name to partici pate in his work of creation, each in his or her own way. We *all* have vocations. Marriage is a vocation. Parenthood is a vocation. It's no accident that most priests and religious emerge from believing, practicing, loving Catholic families. In fact, in many ways, the love between a husband and wife is the foundation stone upon which every other Christian vocation is built. Strong marriages and families make a vital, joy-filled Church. The opposite is also true: Families who are lukewarm in their love for God and indifferent in their worship weaken every other dimension of Catholic life. That's why the Church so urgently needs men and women who can provide the example and guidance our families need.

You'll find that Christopher West is exactly that kind of man: articulate, joyful, faithful to the Church, and absolutely passionate about Jesus Christ and the Gospel. As a husband and father, he writes from experience. He knows the pressures and joys of married life. He knows the objections to Catholic teaching firsthand, because he struggled through them himself. He has the marvelous gift of making important truths easily accessible—demonstrating the "whys" behind the "whats" of

Catholic teaching in fresh and persuasive ways.

Surely the most tender and exhilarating bond in married love is sexual intimacy. It's also the most easily misunderstood and misdirected. That's why the witness of a person like Christopher West is so valuable. In *Good News About Sex and Marriage*, he takes John Paul II's "theology of the body" and makes it understandable, compelling and relevant for married couples today. His reflections on the Church and contraception are simply outstanding. In effect, this little volume is a kind of "catechism of Catholic teaching on sex and marriage"—and therefore perfect for marriage prep courses, RCIA, adult education, and marriage enrichment.

But it's not a theoretical work, nor a textbook. Rather, it's a source of *practical nourishment*, because it continually shows that dealing honestly with issues of sex and marriage brings us face to face with the whole Gospel message and the meaning of our lives. It's entitled *Good News* for a very good reason. It's a book about our humanity, and the human drama of our creation, fall, and redemption in Jesus Christ, which truly is *good* news—good news because there's real power in Christ to live the truth.

Do the Church—and yourself—a favor: Read and reread this book. Encourage everyone you know to do the same.

If you want to do something about the "vocations crisis" ... you can begin right here.

Charles J. Chaput, O.F.M. Cap.
Archbishop of Denver, Colorado

Acknowledgements

I'm very grateful to the following men and women who have helped make this book a reality:

- Pope John Paul II, without whose wisdom this book simply would not exist;
- all my professors at the John Paul II Institute, for the knowledge they passed on to me, especially William May, Lorenzo Albacete, David Schindler, Mary Shivanandan, Stanislaw Grygiel, and Robin Maas;
- all the staff at Servant Publications, especially Bert Ghezzi, for the faith he's had in me since the day I introduced this book idea to him, and Paul Thigpen, for his help editing my manuscript;
- Archbishop Chaput, for writing the foreword and encouraging me in my work;
- Fran Maier, for promoting my work;
- Rebecca Knoell and Helena Diaz, for helping with research;
- Jeanette Stackhouse, for reading and critiquing each chapter as it was written;
- Fr. James Moreno, for his help with the canon law section;
- Michael Kowalewski, for his research on early feminism;
- David Morrison, for his help with chapter eight;
- William May, Fr. Richard Hogan, and Fr. Gerard Beigel for helping to fine tune the final manuscript;
- Greg Weidman, for his comments on and proofing of the entire text;
- and Wendy West, for adding "feminine balance" to my masculine perspective.

Introduction

Man cannot live without love. He remains a being that is incomprehensible for himself, his life is senseless, if love is not revealed to him, if he does not encounter love, if he does not experience it and make it his own, if he does not participate intimately in it. This is why Christ the Redeemer "fully reveals Man to himself."

Pope John Paul II[1]

Growing up in the Catholic Church in the 1970s and 80s, I had plenty of questions about, and objections to, the Church's teachings on sex and marriage. When my hormones kicked in, just about everything I'd been taught about "staying pure" went out the window. Over the next several years, though, my sexual behavior would take its toll on me.

As a freshman in college, I found myself deeply and painfully confused about my own identity as a man. I couldn't deny the fact that I'd brought much of this pain and confusion upon myself through my sexual attitudes and behaviors. The rampant promiscuity of college dorm life only served to magnify the meaninglessness of it all.

The stories of "sexual conquest" that we all shared (and no doubt exaggerated) as freshman guys made me think more and more about the ugliness of which men are capable. For every "conquest" there was a woman on the other end used and discarded. But no one seemed to care.

It all came to a head for me the night I witnessed a date rape in one of the dorms. (This was a Catholic college, by the way.) The experience haunted me: How could a man treat a woman as nothing but a "thing" for his sexual kicks? But the more I asked myself this question in reference to what I'd witnessed, the more I knew I had to direct that same question toward myself.

I've never raped anybody, I thought. *But am I much different from that guy in the way I've treated women in my own thoughts and attitudes? Don't I also use my girlfriend for my sexual kicks?* When I was

13

finally honest with myself, I had to conclude that I wasn't much better than the rapist.

In this time of deep soul searching, I became angry with God. "You gave men these hormones!" I insisted. "They seem to be getting me and everybody else I know in a heck of a lot of trouble. What am I supposed to do with them? I want to know the truth! What's this sex thing all about? What does it mean to be a man?"

That prayer set me on a quest to discover the truth about sex. Christ said, "Seek, and you will find" (Mt 7:7). So I sought.

To make a long story short, what I ultimately found were the writings of Pope John Paul II. Here is a man who has rethought and re-presented the teachings of the Church on sex and marriage with profound insight and great originality. His work sets the stage for a new "sexual revolution" that promises to deliver what its precursor couldn't: the true satisfaction of the desire that drives us all—to love and be loved.

In fact, John Paul's contributions to the Church's teachings on sex and marriage are so vast that over two-thirds of what the Catholic Church has ever said on these subjects has come from his pontificate. Yet his work is virtually unknown to the average Catholic. When his insights are given the recognition they deserve, our world will see the restoration of marriage and the family and the building of a true culture of life. This, I believe, will be the new springtime of which he so often speaks.

In the space of a few months I devoured the Holy Father's *Theology of the Body*,[2] his Apostolic Exhortation *On the Christian Family in the Modern World (Familiaris Consortio)*,[3] and his book *Love and Responsibility*.[4] What I read dissected my heart. Somehow, this celibate old pontiff was able to put his finger on the deepest stirrings of my being and help me make sense out of them.

He was able to explain the *whys* behind the *whats* of Catholic teaching in a way that showed the profound beauty of God's reason for creating us male and female in the first place. He radically altered the way I saw myself as a man, the way I looked upon women, the way I understood the Church and God. In short, he changed my view of, well, *everything*. I knew then that I would spend the rest of my life studying this pope's thought and sharing it with others.

Now, as a full-time educator focusing on Church teaching about sex and marriage, I speak to a variety of audiences about these issues on a regular basis. Everywhere I go, people ask sincere, pointed questions about the Church's teaching. They raise issues and objections that weigh heavily on their hearts and intimately affect their own lives and the lives of those they love. Such questions and objections deserve sincere, direct, and thorough responses—responses that address this most intimate area of human life head-on in a way that helps people make sense of seemingly "arbitrary" or "antiquated" Church teachings.

Inevitably, as I draw from my own experience and what I've learned from John Paul II to explain the Church's teaching, people respond: "I went to Catholic schools my whole life and never heard this. Why not?" Others respond in tears: "If I had only known this earlier in my life, perhaps I would have been spared the pain of so many mistakes."

This book was born out of these exchanges. It's a book that people like yourself have helped me to write. I've gathered together questions and objections from single adults, engaged couples, newly married couples, couples who have been married ten, twenty, even forty or more years; from Catholics, Protestants, and unbelievers; from those who are happily and unhappily married, and from those who have suffered the pain of divorce. I present them all here and address them one by one.

Following John Paul's lead, chapter one lays the biblical foundations for God's plan for sex and marriage. Subsequent chapters are divided topically and presented in a question-and-answer format. The aim is to be as comprehensive as possible in terms of what people want to know. Even if you have a question that isn't directly addressed, you can gain the tools necessary to arrive at an educated Catholic response.

Some readers might want to look up answers to specific questions for quick reference. That's fine, but keep in mind that each chapter builds on the previous one. To get the full picture, you should proceed chapter by chapter. I'd also strongly recommend taking the time to read the endnotes. Besides references, they often contain helpful information, including additional resources and how to order them.

It's my heartfelt prayer that, whatever your state and stage in life, this book will help you in your quest to know, understand, live, and experience the beautiful truth about human love. For that's where we find the image of the divine, a foretaste of heaven—the consummate satisfaction of all our most intimate longings.

Christopher West

One

The Great Mystery
Laying the Foundation

The "great mystery," which is the Church and humanity in Christ, does not exist apart from the "great mystery" expressed in the "one flesh" ... reality of marriage and the family.

Pope John Paul II[1]

The Church's teaching on sex and marriage is *good news*. This truth must be emphasized from the start. It's good news because it's the truth about love, and true love is the fulfillment of the human person.

But the Church's teaching on sex and marriage is also *challenging* news. This is so because the truth about love is always challenging.

When we search out the true meaning of sexuality, we touch on the core of our being as men and women. We encounter our deepest longings and aspirations and, at the same time, our deepest fears, wounds, selfishness, and sins. Here lies the challenge: we must face the reality of our humanity—the good and the bad—if we are to discover the truth about our sexuality. Inevitably this leads us to the cross. For it is Christ who, by showing us the truth about love, shows us the meaning of life.

"Love one another as I have loved you" (Jn 15:12). These words of Christ sum up the meaning of life *and* the meaning of human sexuality. At its core, sexual morality is about expressing God's love through our bodies. This is why Pope John Paul II can say that if we live according to the truth of our sexuality, we fulfill the very meaning of our being and existence.[2]

The opposite, however, is also true. If we don't live according to the truth of our sexuality, we miss the meaning of our existence altogether. We forfeit true joy, true happiness.

Disputes about sexual morality, then, are not merely about differing ethical perspectives, different interpretations of Scripture, or Church authority versus personal conscience. No, they go much deeper than that. At their root, disputes about sexual morality are disputes about the very meaning of life.

The Church never fails to proclaim that Christ came into the world not only to show us the meaning of life but also to give us the grace to overcome our fears, wounds, selfishness, and sins in order to live life according to that meaning. True love is possible. That's the promise the Church holds out to us in her teachings on sex and marriage. This is good news. This is great news.

But if this is such "great news," you might ask, why do so many people dispute the Church's teaching? Let's be honest here. People find many points about Catholic teaching to dispute, but if someone has a bone to pick with the Catholic Church, it's almost always related to sex. Whether it's Church teaching about contraception ("C'mon, get with the modern world!"), divorce and remarriage ("How insensitive can you get?"), or the ordination of men alone to the priesthood ("Proof positive that the Church is an oppressor of women"), such contentions depend finally on disagreements over our ideas about sex.

That's why it's so important that we come to a clear understanding of what God has revealed to us about the nature of human sexuality. While popular opinion holds that a Christian perspective on sex is downright negative, what we actually discover by reflecting on the Scriptures is that sex in God's plan is more awesome than any human being could possibly dream. It's quite literally *in-credible*—that is, unbelievable. Only faith is able to believe the "great mystery."

The Central Place of Sexuality in God's Plan

Sex, then, is by no means a peripheral issue. In fact, Pope John Paul II says the call to "nuptial love" revealed through our sexuality is "the fundamental element of human existence in the world."[3] It doesn't get more important than that. He even insists that we can't understand Christianity if we don't understand the truth and meaning of our sexuality.[4]

From beginning to end, the Bible itself is a story about marriage. It begins in the Book of Genesis with the marriage of Adam and Eve, and it ends in the Book of Revelation with the "wedding of the Lamb"—the marriage of Christ and the Church. Throughout the Old Testament, God's love for his people is described as the love of a husband for his bride. In the New Testament, Christ *embodies* this love. He comes as the heavenly Bridegroom to unite himself forever to his Bride—to us.

Yes, God's plan from all eternity is to "marry" us—to draw us into closest communion with himself. God wanted to reveal this eternal plan to us in a way we couldn't miss, so he stamped it right in our very being as male and female. This means that everything God wants to tell us on earth about who he is, who we are, the meaning of life, the reason he created us, how we are to live, and even our ultimate destiny is contained somehow in the truth and meaning of sexuality and marriage. This is important stuff.

Let's take a closer look.

Male and Female: Image of the Trinity

The Book of Genesis actually contains two creation accounts. We read in the first account that God created humanity in his image and likeness specifically as male and female (see Gn 1:27). This means that somehow, in the complementarity of the sexes, we image God. As male and female, we make visible God's invisible mystery.

What is God's invisible mystery? St. John sums it up well: "God is love" (1 Jn 4:8). We often think of this verse in terms of God's love for us. That's part of its meaning. But even before God's love for us, he is love *in himself*, in the relationship of the three Persons of the Trinity.

God is in himself a life-giving *Communion of Persons*. The Father, from all eternity, is making a gift of himself in love to the Son. (As we read in the Scriptures, Jesus is the "beloved" of the Father; see Mt 3:17.) And the Son, eternally receiving the gift of the Father, makes a gift of himself back to him. The love between them is so real, so profound, that this love *is* another eternal Person—the Holy Spirit.

Among other things, this is what our being made in the image and likeness of God reveals: we're called to love as God loves, in a life-giving *communion of persons*. And we do this specifically as male and female. The man is disposed in his very being toward making the gift of himself to the woman. And the woman is disposed in her very being toward receiving the gift of the man into herself and giving herself back to him. And the love between them is so real, so profound, that, God willing, it may become another human person.

Thus sexual intercourse itself is meant to participate in the very life and love of God. Sexual intercourse itself reveals (makes visible) the invisible mystery of God.[5]

To love and be loved as God loves—this is the deepest desire of the human heart. God put it there when he made us in his image. Nothing else can satisfy. Nothing else will fulfill.

This is what we embody as male and female. Sex is so beautiful, so wonderful, so glorious, that it's meant to express God's free, total, faithful, and fruitful love. Another name for this kind of love is marriage.

Yes—sex is meant to express wedding vows. It's where the words of the wedding vows become flesh. That's why sexual intercourse is called the marital embrace.

At the altar, bride and groom commit themselves to each other freely, totally, faithfully, and fruitfully until death—these are the canonical promises they make, the promises of fidelity, indissolubility, and openness to children. Then that night, and throughout their marriage, they enact their commitment. They express with their bodies what they expressed at the altar with their minds and hearts. In doing so, they consummate their marriage. That is, they complete it, perfect it, seal it, renew it.

Marriage: Sacrament of Christ and the Church

Spouses not only image the love of God within the Trinity; they also image the love between God and all humanity, made visible in the love of Christ and the Church. By virtue of their baptisms, the marriage of Christians is a sacrament. That means it's a living sign that truly communicates and participates in the union of Christ and the Church. The marriage vows lived out in the spouses' "one flesh" union constitute this living sign.[6]

Paraphrasing St. Paul: For this reason a man will leave father and mother and cling to his bride, and the two shall become one flesh. This is a profound mystery, *and it refers to Christ and the Church* (see Eph 5:31-32). Christ left his Father in heaven. He left the home of his mother on earth—to give up his *body* for his Bride, so that we might become "one flesh" with him.

Where do we become "one flesh" with Christ? Most specifically in the Eucharist. The Eucharist is the sacramental consummation of the marriage between Christ and the Church. And when we receive the body of our heavenly Bridegroom into our own, just like a bride we conceive new life in us— God's very own life. As Christ said, "Unless you eat the flesh of the Son of man and drink his blood, you have no life in you" (Jn 6:53).

Since the "one flesh" communion of man and wife foreshadowed the Eucharistic communion of Christ and the Church right from the beginning, John Paul II speaks of marriage as the "primordial sacrament." Let's pause for a moment to let this reality sink in. Of all the ways that God chooses to reveal his life and love in the created world, John Paul II is saying, marriage—enacted and consummated by sexual union—is the most fundamental.

St. Paul wasn't kidding when he said this is a "profound mystery." Could God have made our sexuality any more important than this? any more beautiful? any more glorious? God gave us sexual desire itself to be the power to love as he loves, so that we could participate in divine life and fulfill the very meaning of our being and existence.

Sounds great, you say, but it's a far cry from the way sex plays itself out in the experience of real human beings. Yes, it is. The historic abuse of women at the hands of men; the tragedy of rape and other heinous sex crimes, even against children; AIDS and a host of other sexually transmitted diseases; unwed mothers; "fatherless" children; abortion; adultery; skyrocketing divorce rates; prostitution; a multibillion-dollar pornography industry; the general cloud of shame and guilt that hangs over sexual matters—all of this paints a very different picture from the one St. Paul and John Paul II give us.

The picture it paints, in fact, is the tragedy of human sinfulness and our fall from God's intention for our sexuality "in the beginning."

Human Sexuality "in the Beginning"

Back to the Book of Genesis. While the first creation story gives an objective account of our call to love, the second creation story speaks of our first parents' subjective experience of that call. Adam and Eve represent us all. If we allow the inspired Word to speak to us, we see in their story the inner movements of our own hearts being laid bare. We experience an "echo" of God's original intention deep within us. We sense its beauty, realize how far we've fallen from it, and long for its restoration.[7]

God created Adam from the dust of the ground and breathed the breath of life into him (see Gn 2:7).[8] The Hebrew word for "breath" in the original biblical language is also a word for spirit. And let's remember that the Spirit of God is the very love between the Father and the Son. God is breathing *his love* into the man.

What this means, as we've seen, is that the man is a person called to live in a relationship of love with God. The man, having received the love of God, is called to give himself back to God. He's also called to share the love of God with others (see Mt 22:37-40). It's stamped in his very being, and he can only fulfill himself by doing so. As the Second Vatican Council put it, "Man, who is the only creature on earth that God created for his own sake, cannot fully find himself except through the sincere gift of himself."⁹

Not Good to Be Alone

This is why the Lord said, "It is not good that the man should be alone; I will make him a helper fit for him" (Gn 2:18). That is, God said: "I will make someone he can love." So the Lord created animals from the dust of the ground and brought them to the man for him to name.

In naming the animals, he realized he was different from them. The animals weren't free to determine their own actions as he was. They weren't called to love in the image of God as he was. We can imagine Adam's reply to God: "Thanks, God, for all these animals. But I can't love a giraffe. I can't give myself to a fruit fly."

So the Lord put the man into a deep sleep and took a rib from his side. Yet again, we lose some things in the English translation. "Deep sleep" might better be translated "ecstasy." Ecstasy literally means "to go out of oneself," and Adam's "ecstasy" is that God takes a woman *out of himself*. Furthermore, in the original language, the word "rib" is a play on the word "life." That's to say, the woman comes from the very same *life* as the man.¹⁰

What's the life of the man? It was the breath of God that made Adam a living being (see Gn 2:7). Man and woman share a common humanity. *Both* have God's Spirit within them, which means *both* are called to love in the image of God.

Now imagine Adam's state of mind when he awoke to the sight of the woman. The deepest desire of his heart is to give himself away in love to another person "like himself," and he has just finished naming billions of animals and found no one. So what does he say?

"At last, you are the one! You are bone of my bone and flesh of my flesh" (see Gn 2:23). That is, "At last, a person like myself that I can love."

How does Adam know that she's the one he can love? Remember that they were naked. It was their *bodies* that revealed the spiritual truth of their persons. In their nakedness they discovered what John Paul II calls the "nuptial meaning of the body," that is, "the [body's] capacity of expressing love: that love precisely in which the person becomes a gift and—by means of this gift—fulfills the very meaning of his being and existence."¹¹

Adam looked at himself; he looked at Eve. He realized this profound reality: "We go together. God made us *for* each other. I can give myself to you, and you can give yourself to me, and we can live in a life-giving communion of love"—

the image of God, marriage.

That was the sentiment of sexual desire as God created it and as they experienced it: to make a gift of themselves to each other in the image of God. This is why they were naked and felt no shame (see Gn 2:25). There's no shame in loving as God loves, only the experience of joy, peace, and a deep knowledge of human goodness.

The Effects of Original Sin

Let's think about this situation for a moment. If the "one flesh" union of marriage is meant to be the fundamental revelation in creation of God's own life and love, and if there's an enemy of God who wants to keep us from experiencing God's life and love, how might he go about keeping us from it? Hmm ... let's take a look.

God had told Adam that he was free to eat from any tree in the garden except the "tree of the knowledge of good and evil." If he did, he would die (see Gn 2:17). In the symbolism of biblical language, here we see God drawing a line that humanity is not free to cross. God alone knows what is best for us. As creatures, we must trust in God's providence and not seek to determine good and evil for ourselves. If we do, we will die.

Here's an analogy. Suppose you just purchased a new car and are pulling into the gas station to fill it up for the first time. The sticker by the gas tank reads "unleaded gas only."

Now, the person that designed the car knows it inside and out. He knows what's best for it. It would be foolish to say, "I don't care what the manufacturer says. I'm stickin' diesel in here." If you did so, you would have some major car troubles.

Just as it is with the car, the only way our lives will "run" the way they're meant to run is if we live according to the Designer's plan. The sticker on the car isn't meant to limit our freedom but to facilitate our freedom in making good choices. It's the same with God's commands. They serve our freedom.

True freedom is not to do whatever I want. True freedom is to do whatever's good, whatever's in keeping with the truth of our humanity. As Jesus said, it's the truth that sets us free (see Jn 8:32).

But how tempting is the thought of determining for ourselves how we are to live. "I don't care what God says. I don't care that he established a Church to teach the truth. I'm gonna do what *I* want to do." If we recognize this tendency in ourselves, then we recognize that we've inherited original sin.

But why would we ever doubt God's love and provision for us? Why would we ever have eaten from the tree from which God, in his love for us, told us not to eat? Remember: this is just as stupid as putting diesel fuel in an unleaded engine.

Why would we do it? Because, as the *Catechism of the Catholic Church* puts it, "behind the disobedient choice of our first parents lurks a seductive voice, opposed to God, which makes them fall into death out of envy."[12]

This seductive voice is the Father of Lies, the deceiver, Satan. He is envious of the fact that humanity is created in God's own image and likeness and is called as male and female to share in divine life. So Satan sets out to keep us from God's life by convincing us that God doesn't love us.

Placing doubt in the woman's mind, the serpent says: "Did God say, 'You shall not eat of any tree of the garden'?... You will not die. For God knows that when you eat of it your eyes will be opened, and you will be like God, knowing good and evil" (Gn 3:1, 4-5). The implication: God doesn't want you to be like him; God is withholding himself from you; God is not love. If you want to be "like God," then you have to reach out and grasp it for yourself.

Now, wait a minute. God had already created them in his image and *likeness* (see Gn 1:26). Satan's trying to sell them something they already have.

When the woman saw that the fruit was "pleasing to the eye," she took some and ate it. She gave some to her husband, and he ate it. Then their eyes were opened, and they realized they were naked, so they covered themselves (see Gn 3:6-7).

What's happened here? Before they ate the fruit they were both naked and felt no shame. Now their experience of nakedness changed. Why?

God, who is Truth, cannot tell a lie. He said that if they ate from the tree they would die. Now, they didn't immediately fall over dead, but they did die spiritually.

It was the Spirit that was given to them as the calling and the power to love. When the Spirit "died" in our first parents, so did their ready ability to love in the image of God as male and female. Absent the Spirit, sexual desire became inverted, self-seeking.

Adam and Eve no longer clearly saw in each other's bodies the revelation of God's plan of love. They each now saw the other's body more as a thing to use for their own selfish desires. In this way the experience of nakedness in the presence of the other—and in the presence of God—became an experience of fear, alienation, shame: "I was afraid, because I was naked; and I hid myself" (Gn 3:10).

Their shame was connected not so much with the body itself but with the lust now in their hearts. For they still knew that since they were created as persons for their own sakes, they were never meant to be looked upon as things for another person's use. So they covered their bodies to protect their own dignity from the other's lustful "look." This is, in fact, a positive function of shame, because it actually serves to protect the "nuptial meaning of the body."

Sexual Complementarity Becomes Sexual Discord

The body is the revelation of the person, as John Paul II puts it.[13] This means that all our differences as men and women (emotional, mental, spiritual, as well as physical) were created by God to complement each other, to unite us in life-giving ways. Because of sin, however, we often experience these differences as the cause of great tension, conflict, and division. Indeed, history tells the tale of the chaos that original sin has brought into man and woman's relationship.

Initially, Adam received Eve as the true blessing and gift from God that she is. But after sin, he was blaming her for all his problems. He even faulted God, saying, "The woman *you* put here with me—*she* gave me the fruit" (see Gn 3:12). It's all *her* fault. How often do men, even today, blame and resent women for their own problems?

Furthermore, women throughout history have suffered greatly because of the dominance of men. "Your desire shall be for your husband, and he shall rule over you" (Gn 3:16): This is not God's intention. This is a result of sin. But some men, refusing to face their own sinfulness, even try to use various Scripture verses to justify their dominance (see, for example, chapter three, question 16).

But let's remember that it's a two-way street. Fallen woman's "desire for her husband" has also been a source of angst for men. While men often dominate and manipulate women for their own physical gratification, women often use their "feminine wiles" to manipulate men as well—perhaps more for emotional gratification.[14] As the common observation goes, men will use love to get sex, and women will use sex to get love.

It's important to realize that even though we may be tempted to think men's perversions are uglier than women's, each, in its own way, is a serious distortion of authentic sexual love. Both treat the other not as a person created for his or her own sake but as a thing to be used for selfish gratification.

Such gratification at the expense of others—like diesel fuel in an unleaded-only engine—always causes serious "car troubles."

The Redemption of Our Sexuality in Christ

While an echo of God's original intention remains in our hearts, this distorted way of relating has become our lot. Tragically, for many people, it's all they know. They simply accept it as the norm. After all, "men will be men," and "women will always play the temptress," right?

Wrong! Christ came to restore God's original intention of love in the world. This is the good news of the gospel. Through an ongoing conversion of heart we can experience the redemption of our sexuality.

This is what Christ was calling us to in the Sermon on the Mount when he said: "Everyone who looks at a woman lustfully has already committed adultery with her in his heart" (Mt 5:28). Of course, his words apply to men and women equally. As if to emphasize the seriousness of this sin, he immediately added, "If your right eye causes you to sin, pluck it out.... And if your right hand causes you to sin, cut it off.... It is better that you lose one of your members than that your whole body go into hell" (Mt 5:29-30).

Hell is the absence of God's love. So is lust. That's why it's so serious.

So what are we to do? If we look at the common human experience, it seems that everyone is condemned by Christ's words. That's true. But let's remember, Christ came into the world not to condemn us. He came to save us (see Jn 3:16-18).

Reflecting on these words of Christ, John Paul II poses the question: "Are we to fear the severity of [Christ's] words, or rather have confidence in their salvific content, in their power?"[15] Their power lies in the fact that the man who utters them is "the Lamb of God, who takes away the sin of the world" (Jn 1:29).

How does he do it? By making a total, faithful, and fruitful gift of his body to his Bride, the Church, on the cross. And by once again breathing the Spirit upon humanity (see Jn 20:22).

Paraphrasing John Paul II, sin and death entered human history, in a way, through the very heart of the unity of the first Adam and Eve.[16] Similarly, redemption and new life entered human history through the very heart of the unity of the New Adam and Eve, that is, Christ and the Church. Right after Adam and Eve fell, we have the foretelling of this redemption in a Scripture passage known as the *Protoevangelium* (the first announcement of the gospel). Speaking to the serpent, God says: "I will put enmity between you and the woman, and between your seed and her seed; he shall bruise your head, and you shall bruise his heel" (Gn 3:15).

Jesus is the New Adam, the offspring of "the woman" who will deliver the fatal blow to the serpent's head. As the model of the Bride-Church, Mary represents the New Eve.[17] Christ's redemptive "marriage" to the Church is foreshadowed at the wedding feast of Cana (see Jn 2:1-11) and consummated on the cross at Calvary.[18]

When Mary came to Jesus to tell him that the wedding feast was out of wine, Jesus said, "O woman, what have you to do with me? My hour has not yet come" (Jn 2:4). Already, Jesus is referring to the hour of his passion.

The water changed to wine at Cana prefigures the blood and water that flow from Christ's side at Calvary (see Jn 19:34). As figures of baptism and the Eucharist, the blood and water symbolize the very life of God coming from the side of the New Adam as the birth of the New Eve. (Remember that the word "rib" used in Genesis was a play on the word "life.") And like the first Adam, the New Adam calls her by name—"woman" (see Gn 2:23 and Jn 19:26).

Creation is, as theologians would say, recapitulated—that is, repeated, summed up—in the work of Christ. Man and woman have been born again. Their perennial love for one another has been re-created. (See the chart below.)

First Adam and Eve	*New Adam and Eve*
Adam put into deep sleep	Christ put into "deep sleep" on the cross
Eve comes from his side	Church born of his side in blood and water
Eve is given a message by the angel Lucifer to deny God's life.	Mary is given a message by the angel Gabriel to receive God's life.
God's life dies within her (us)	God's life is conceived within her (us)
They denied the gift of God's love and were unable to love others	They believed in the gift of God's love and are able to love others
Their union transmitted original sin to all humanity	Their union brings the new life of redemption to all humanity

"The woman" at the foot of the cross represents us all, men and women. We are *all* called to be the Bride of Christ.[19] In offering us his body, Christ offers us a "marriage proposal." All we need do is say yes by offering our bodies—our whole selves—back to him. This is what the sacramental life of the Church is all about.

In fact, the *Catechism* describes baptism as a "nuptial bath."[20] Here, as we unite ourselves with Christ's sacrifice, we're cleansed of our sin by the washing with water through the word (see Eph 5:26). Furthermore, having already been united (or married) to him in baptism, when we receive Christ's body in the Eucharist, we consummate our marriage, and, as stated earlier, we conceive new life in us—life in the Holy Spirit.

As much as lust blinds man and woman to their own truth and distorts their sexual desires, so much does this new life in the Holy Spirit empower men and women to love one another as they were called to in the beginning. Through the sacraments we can know and experience the transforming power of Christ's love.

This is good news. This is great news. Yes, we've put the wrong gas in our engines and suffered the consequent car troubles. But God doesn't say, "You idiot. I told you so." No! In his infinite mercy he offers us an engine overhaul and all the free unleaded gas we could ever need. He doesn't leave us to wallow in our sin but offers us redemption. All we need do, like a bride, is receive this great gift.

A Question of Faith

It makes sense that, since it was man and woman's turning away from God that distorted their relationship in the first place, restoring the truth and meaning of human sexuality requires a radical *re-turn* to God. Satan convinced us in the beginning that God doesn't love us, that he's withholding himself from us. In order to dispel all doubt, God became one of us and made an everlasting gift of himself to us on the cross.

Each of us, then, needs to ask him or herself: *Do I believe in God's gift? Do I believe in his infinite love for me?*

Living the truth about our sexuality is thus really a question of faith. Do we believe the gospel or not? We confess that Christ came to save us from sin and reconcile us to the Father. Yet this may simply rattle off our tongues without much thought.

Ask yourself: *Do I really believe that Christ came to save me from sin? Do I really believe that, with the help of God's grace, it's possible to overcome my weaknesses, selfishness, and lust in order to love others as Christ has loved me? In other words, do I really believe that Christ can redeem me—even my sexuality?*

Resisting the sinful distortions of sexual desire and living in accordance with the truth is a very difficult struggle, even for someone with a solid moral formation. In a sense, this struggle brings us to the heart of the spiritual battle (see Eph 6:12) that we must fight as Christians if we are to resist evil—both in the world and in ourselves—and love others as Christ has loved us. Winning this battle takes faith in Christ, dedication, commitment, honesty with ourselves and others, and a willingness to make sacrifices and deny our own selfish desires. But love is not afraid of those things; love *is* those things.

Yes, the Church's teaching about sex is challenging. It's the challenge of the gospel itself, the challenge to *believe* in Christ and pick up our crosses to follow him. Yes, we are weak. On our own we have no hope of meeting the challenge.

But to whom is this challenge given? To men and women who remain slaves to their weaknesses? No! To men and women who have been set free to love by the power of the cross.[21] Let's not empty the cross of its power, but let's believe in the good news. Let's believe that in Christ, true love—that love that is the very meaning of our being and existence—is possible. This is what the Church never ceases to proclaim to every man and woman.

God's Original Plan: The Norm for Sex and Marriage

When questioned about divorce, Christ pointed his followers back to God's original plan. "For your hardness of heart [i.e., sin] Moses allowed you to divorce your wives, but from the beginning [before sin] it was not so" (Mt 19:8). Because Christ takes away our sin, he is able to restore God's original plan of love as the norm for marriage and all sexual expression.

This means marriage is only marriage, and sex is only sex, to the extent that they participate in God's free, total, faithful, and fruitful love. This norm—God's original plan of love prior to sin—is the proper basis for addressing all the many questions and objections that people are posing today about the Church's teaching on sexual morality and marriage.

Two

Who Says?

Church Authority and
Other Preliminary Questions

*No man is so free as he who is able to renounce his own will and
do the will of God.*

Author unknown

People hate being told what to do and what not to do, especially when it
comes to sex. Part of this attitude bears witness to our dignity as free
human beings. When we're *forced* to do something, we often sense that it violates our dignity.

Yet, another aspect of this attitude bears witness to the reality of original
sin. We don't want anyone, not even God, telling us that something we want
to do is wrong. We want to determine what is good and evil for ourselves. It's
the problem of pride.

Human pride rebels against authority. And when authority is abused, we
should protest. But when authority is exercised according to God's own design,
if we want to be truly free, then we must obey it. It's the paradox of the gospel:
by dying, we live (see Jn 12:24); by giving ourselves away we find ourselves (see
Mt 16:25); by obeying the truth we're set free (see Jn 8:32).

Obedience at its best doesn't stem from force or fear but from love for the
good, the true, and the beautiful—love for God. Freedom is not doing whatever
I want. Freedom is doing whatever is good. Freedom is doing God's will.

But how do we know God's will, especially with regard to our sexuality? It
simply wouldn't make sense for God to hold us accountable to his will if we
didn't have a sure way of knowing what it is. In this lies the good news of the
Church's teaching: God has revealed his will to us.

With that in mind, let's consider some of the most frequent questions asked
about the Church's teaching authority—questions that must be answered

31

before we can deal with what the Church teaches specifically about human sexuality.

1. Who determines what the Church officially teaches? Aren't we all "the Church"?

The Church is united to Christ as a bride to her husband. It's Christ who determines what his Bride teaches. Christ gave authority to some members of the Church to be faithful witnesses of all that he has commanded; this is the role of the Church's Magisterium. This official teaching office is made up of the pope and the bishops throughout the world who are in union with him. When the pope teaches on issues of faith and morals, and when the bishops teach on faith and morals in union with him, they teach in Christ's name and with his authority.

Yes, all baptized Catholics make up the Catholic Church. We are all "one body" in Christ (see 1 Cor 12:12). This body, however, has a sacred order to it, a *hierarchy* ("hier-archy" literally means "sacred order"). As St. Paul said, the body of Christ has different members who play different roles (see 1 Cor 12). All these different roles are vital to the organic functioning of the body: "The eye cannot say to the hand, 'I have no need of you,' nor again the head to the feet, 'I have no need of you'" (1 Cor 12:21). Nor should the eye wish she were a hand, nor the foot wish he were the head.

Those in the Church who teach with the authority of Christ don't claim the task for themselves. They are ordained by God to do so. That's their role within the body. The Magisterium, then, is a tremendous gift to the Church and the world because it gives us a sure way of knowing the teachings of Christ.

2. Where did the Church get the idea of having a "Magisterium" to give official teachings?

Christ founded his Church upon St. Peter, the leader of the apostles. He gave Peter "the keys of the kingdom of heaven" and told him: "Whatever you bind on earth shall be bound in heaven, and whatever you loose on earth shall be loosed in heaven" (see Mt 16:13-20 for the whole discourse).

In other words, Christ gave St. Peter the authority to represent him on earth, to teach in his name and with his authority. This wasn't because Peter was an impeccable guy, but because Christ would protect him and the other apostles by sending them the Holy Spirit to guide them into "all truth" (see Jn 16:13).

What Christ promised two thousand years ago continues in our own day.

The pope and the bishops are in a direct, traceable line of succession from St. Peter and the other apostles—hence we speak of the one, holy, catholic, and *apostolic* Church. They too are promised the gift of the Holy Spirit to guide the Church into all truth. So as Catholics we believe that when they teach on matters of faith and morals, they do so with the authority of Christ himself.[1]

Led by the pope, the Church is "the pillar and bulwark of the truth" (1 Tm 3:15). This isn't because of human merit but because the Church remains in the most intimate union with her Bridegroom, Jesus Christ. Jesus said to his apostles, "He who hears you hears me, and he who rejects you rejects me" (Lk 10:16). Thus the Second Vatican Council can teach that when we receive the teachings of the pope and bishops and live according to them, we are receiving "not the mere word of men, but truly the word of God" (see 1 Thes 2:13).[2]

3. Are you saying the Church actually believes she speaks for God and knows "the truth"? That's so arrogant!

Yes, the Church actually believes she speaks for God and has been granted by Christ a share in his own infallibility.[3] That's an amazingly bold claim with which we all must seriously reckon. We can draw only one of two conclusions: Either the Church is extremely arrogant—or, just maybe, she's right.

In the end, there's no middle ground. If the Church is right, then we will see her as a great blessing from God, and we will want to conform our lives to what she teaches. Even when we may not understand a certain *why* behind a teaching, we will trust that it will come to light in due time. On the other hand, if the Church is extremely arrogant, then we should not even want to be associated with the name Catholic.

This is a weighty reality. It confronts us and forces us to choose. We live in a culture that teaches us to avoid such ultimate choices. We prefer to invent both/and scenarios rather than face up to the inescapable either/or realities of life.

In other words, we live in a culture that rejects objective truth. "That may be true for you, but not for me," people say. Or, "Anybody's opinion is just as valid as anyone else's." We've all been affected by these attitudes.

But Jesus taught something very different. He taught that he is the truth (see Jn 14:6), and he established a Church that he promised would teach the truth (see Jn 16:13). He calls us to accept that. We are free not to accept it. But it's a terribly weighty decision that we dare not take lightly.

Approaching the matter from a purely practical perspective, it only makes sense that Christ would establish a definitive authority on earth to make his will known. Otherwise, interpreting Scripture and determining God's will on issues with eternal consequences would amount to a guessing game. A God-given authority on earth is essential to maintain unity in faith.

If Christ truly gave this authority to the Catholic Church, it's not arrogant for her to exercise it. If we're honest, what's arrogant is for us to think we know better than the Church what God's will is in matters of faith and morals.

4. How can the Church claim to teach without error? History shows that the Church has made lots of mistakes and done some horrible things. What about Galileo, the Crusades, and the Inquisition?

On the first Sunday of Lent, 2000, John Paul II publicly sought God's mercy and forgiveness for the past sins committed by members of the Church. As this gesture so clearly indicates, the Church doesn't claim that all her members and leaders throughout history have never spoken in error or never made mistakes. (As a member of the Church, have you ever made a mistake or spoken in error? Blows that theory ...) The charism that protects the Church from error applies to her definitive teachings on matters of *faith* and *morals*.

Certainly members of the Church, including some priests, bishops, and popes, have not always lived according to the teachings of their own faith. They have made mistakes. At times, terrible things have been done in the name of "the Church."

This is scandalous and can weaken people's faith in the Church. Yet the fact that the Church has endured so much corruption and is still standing after two thousand years also bears testimony to Christ's words when he founded the Church upon Peter: "The powers of death shall not prevail against [the Church]" (Mt 16:18).

Why has there been corruption in the Church? First of all because the Church is made up of people such as you and me. As the saying goes, the Church is not a "hotel for saints," it's a "hospital for sinners." Yes, we're all called to be saints, but we don't reach perfection in this life. Meanwhile, as Christ said, both wheat and weeds will be growing in the Church until the harvest (see Mt 13:24-30).

But the good news is this: even when individual members of the Church have been unfaithful, even when in certain times of history the weeds have seemed more plentiful than the wheat, Christ has never abandoned his Bride. While members of the Church have made mistakes, the Church has never erred in those teachings on faith and morals that she has proclaimed in a definitive manner, and she never will. This is God's own promise.

5. Doesn't the "infallibility" of the Church only apply in rare pronouncements of the pope?

The Church exercises the charism of infallibility (the inability to err) in two ways. The *extraordinary* way is exercised when the pope makes an *ex cathedra* ("from the chair" of St. Peter) pronouncement.[4] The *ordinary* way is exercised when the Magisterium agrees on a matter of faith or morals as definitively to be held.[5]

It's a common error to think infallibility only applies to *ex cathedra* pronouncements, as if these are the only teachings Catholics "have" to believe. That would mean we wouldn't "have" to believe in the Trinity or the Incarnation or a host of other core beliefs that have never been defined by *ex cathedra* pronouncements. As the *Catechism* makes clear, "The infallibility of the Magisterium ... extends to *all* the elements of doctrine, including moral doctrine, without which the saving truths of the faith cannot be preserved, expounded, or observed."[6]

Furthermore, even in those cases when the Magisterium teaches without exorcising the charism of infallibility, we are called to adhere to those teachings "with religious assent."[7]

6. The Church should get rid of its hierarchical structure and be more democratic and open to dialogue.

In recent times, the term "hierarchy" has become a bad word. Many seem to think it's somehow synonymous with inequality. But as we noted before, hierarchy simply means *sacred order*.

To reject hierarchy, then, is not to reject inequality. To reject hierarchy is to reject God's ordering of the universe. Not a good idea. The opposite of hierarchy is not equality but *anarchy*—no order at all, chaos.[8]

Our world today is filled with chaos, and it all stems from rejecting God-given authority. To a large extent, what has been specifically rejected is God's plan for sex and marriage. It's difficult to find even one social evil, one element of societal chaos, that is not in some way related to the breakdown of marriage and the misuse of sex.

The Church is not a democracy. The truth about Christ and what he teaches cannot be determined by popular vote. If God reveals something to be true, it's not open for "dialogue" about whether or not it's really true.

On the other hand, if by dialogue we mean an open discussion about a given teaching with the goal of understanding *why* the Church teaches what she teaches, that's legitimate. But if by dialogue we mean that the Church needs

to listen to other opinions with the goal of being willing to change her definitive teaching on faith and morals, that's not legitimate. The Church simply
cannot change what the Holy Spirit has revealed to be true. It's not a matter
of stubborn unwillingness; it's a matter of *impossibility*.

For example, it makes no sense to "dialogue" about whether or not $2 + 2 = 4$.
We can "dialogue" about *why* $2 + 2 = 4$ with the goal of explaining it for those
who don't understand, but we can't hope to change the fact that $2 + 2 = 4$.

God does not change for us. We must change for him. How our pride rebels.
But until we come to grips with this fundamental reality—that we are *not*
God—then we're living an illusion.

**7. As a Catholic, am I not allowed to question the Church's teachings? Perhaps
the Church is wrong about some things. Do I have to believe everything the
Church teaches?**

There's nothing wrong when a person growing in his faith poses questions
in an earnest quest for truth. That's how we discover what the truth is. No one,
then, should be afraid of entertaining "perhaps." Perhaps God doesn't exist. But
perhaps he does. Perhaps the Catholic Church is woefully misguided in her
teachings. But perhaps her teachings come from God himself. These kinds of
questions *must* be entertained.

Those who are afraid to put their beliefs to the test in this way are clinging
to an ideology that they fear will not stand up to reality. On the other hand,
those who seek the truth have no fear of surrendering their beliefs to reality.
Entertaining "perhaps" is the only path to the truth. It's the only path to the
surety and freedom of faith.

Faith, however, is a gift that doesn't necessarily come all at once. The
Church herself recognizes that "an educational growth process is necessary in
order that individual believers ... may patiently be led forward arriving at a rich-
er understanding and fuller integration of [Christ's] mystery in their lives."[9]

Still, if the Church is who she claims to be, then the gift of faith will ultimately lead the seeker of truth to embrace all that she teaches. If in the end a
person still protests what the Church teaches, then that person doesn't really
believe the Catholic Church. At that point it would seem hypocritical to
remain Catholic.

"Ask, and it will be given you; seek, and you will find; knock, and it will be
opened to you" (Mt 7:7). Pose every question you've ever had about the Church,
entertain every "perhaps" you can think of, but don't be satisfied until you find
the answers.[10]

8. Isn't morality a matter of my own conscience?

The Church has always taught that Catholics, like all people, are obligated to follow their own consciences—on issues of sexual morality and every other matter. But there is an even more fundamental obligation to *form* the conscience according to the truth. Conscience is not free to *invent* right and wrong. Conscience is called to discover the truth of what is right and wrong and to submit its judgments to the truth once the truth is found.

While all of us have the basic moral law written in our hearts by God, original sin tends to cloud our judgment. Sometimes our own fallen desires can take us completely off track. This is why the conscientious person sees the Church's moral teachings as a tremendous gift. They're a *sure norm* for forming one's conscience according to the truth.

Too often we use "conscience" to give a morally acceptable veneer to what we wanted to do all along without discerning our behavior in light of objective standards. Think about it: if personal conscience is the autonomous determinant of good and evil, morality becomes whatever *I* want it to be. Who are *we*, then, to tell a rapist or a mass murderer that what he does is evil if *his* conscience says it's OK? There must be objective standards that we're all responsible to follow. Those objective standards are given to us by God and are revealed through the teachings of his Church.

Yet, what is frequently our response when we don't like what his Church teaches? We hide behind our claims of "conscience" and imagine a God who accepts what *we* want. But that's a god who is other than God. That's an idol.

We'll never find peace and true happiness until we embrace God's will for our lives. That's what conversion of heart is all about—and we're *all* in need of it.

9. The Church should stop judging people and imposing her teaching on everybody. We should all be free to make our own choices.

We *are* all free to make our own choices. The Church never *imposes* her teaching. But the Church does boldly and fearlessly *propose* her teaching to the world as the truth of what it means to love. We're free to embrace the Church's proposal or reject it. Love can't be forced on anybody.

While it's true that God alone can judge the human heart, we can and must make moral judgments about certain *behaviors*. The Church would betray God and all humanity if she didn't uphold God's will as the objective standard for all. To condemn a person's *behavior*, however, is not to condemn the *person*, but to call that person to embrace the truth of love.

Love isn't arbitrary. Love isn't whatever makes a person "feel good." Love means following Christ and keeping his commandments (see Jn 15:10). This is what the Church's teaching is all about. And it's a joy to live, not a burden.

10. Why is there such a widespread notion that the Church is down on sex?

Even the most loyal Catholic must admit that this generally held notion—even if incorrect—is not merely the fancy of illusion. Far too many impressionable young minds have been formed (or mis-formed) by the prudish, scolding tones of a well-intentioned (we pray) but misguided and sexually disintegrated nun or priest. From where comes this general cloud of "sexual negativity" that seems so closely associated in people's minds with the Catholic Church?

To be sure it has much to do with misinterpretation of Church teaching. But we don't do a disservice to the Church by admitting that it also has much to do with the disparaging treatment of sex that has recurred all too often in the works of various historical Christian authors.

The objective person will admit that a deep ambivalence about the body and its functions, particularly its sexual, genital functions, is not a limited Christian phenomenon but a universal human phenomenon.[11] As such, Christian authors, like many others, have not been exempt from the failure to appreciate fully the goodness and beauty of sex. Still, it's important, within the context of this admission, that we not confuse the mind *of* the Church with the minds of people *in* the Church.

In the face of many attacks, the Church's official teachings have always upheld the inherent goodness of the body and of sexuality. The Church has deemed all contrary systems of thought nothing short of heretical. Unfortunately, until the twentieth century, official pronouncements on the matter have been relatively brief and juridical in nature. As such, they haven't made as lasting an impression on our culture's "historical consciousness" as some of the more extensive writings of Catholic thinkers who were heavily influenced by currents of thought alien to the mind of the Church. Thus, despite significant developments of Magisterial teaching on sex and marriage in the last century, the notion that the Church is "down on sex" still lingers.

Regarding Church teaching itself, it seems that misinterpretation of the esteem accorded the celibate vocation, as well as misinterpretation of the Church's strict moral code, have also contributed to the prevailing attitude.

Traditionally, those who followed Christ's words and chose to remain celibate "for the sake of the kingdom" (Mt 19:12) were considered to have chosen **the** more holy or "higher" path. While there is a proper way of understanding **this** (as we'll discuss in chapter nine), it has often been misunderstood to mean that those who do marry and have sex are somehow less holy, or even "unholy."

The sentiment goes like this: if virginity is so good, sex must be so bad. If refraining from sex makes one pure and holy, having sex must make one dirty and unholy.

Yet nothing could be further from the mind of the Church in promoting the celibate vocation. The Church holds this vocation in such high regard precisely because she holds that which is sacrificed for the sake of God—genital sexual expression—in such high regard. If sex were something unclean and unholy, offering it as a gift to God would be an act of sacrilege. But since sex is one of the most precious treasures God has given humanity, making a gift of it back to God is one of the most genuine expressions of thanksgiving (*eucharistia*) for such a great gift. The other is receiving it from God's hands and living it as the expression of the marital covenant.

The misinterpretation of the Church's strict moral code is similar. The sentiment goes like this: if the Church says you can't do this and you can't do that—everything that it seems people *want* to do—then the Church *must* think sex is bad, even if she grants the one reluctant exception of "doing it" for the purpose of procreation. This latter belief (that the Church teaches you can only have sex if you want a baby) is a fallacy we'll get to in chapters five and six.

For the present, we must clarify the simple fact that saying, "Handle with care"—or even "Handle with *extreme* care"—is in no way synonymous with saying, "This is bad." In fact, what are those things in life that we handle with the most care? The things that have the most inherent value. It's because sex is so valuable, because it's so precious in the eyes of Christ and his Church, that it must be handled with extreme care.

When we venture into the realm of sex, we are on holy ground. Only those who are properly disposed can handle the mystery.

There's a parallel here with another holy mystery of the Church: the Eucharist. The Church has many "strict" teachings about who can and cannot receive the Eucharist, how it's to be received, and with what spiritual dispositions. It would be absurd to conclude that the Church is therefore "down on the Eucharist." It's no less absurd to conclude that the Church is down on sex because of her strict moral teaching about it.[12]

Historically speaking, God tends to grant the Church what she needs when she needs it. Not until the twentieth century, with its widespread dismissal of long-held sexual mores, did the Church have "need" to deepen her understanding of conjugal love, sex, and marriage beyond her previous brief pronouncements. Hence, as noted before, over two-thirds of what the Catholic Church has ever officially said about sex and marriage has come from Pope John Paul II.

Granted, the Church tends to move slowly. But once this Pope's profound rethinking of the Church's teaching has been assimilated into the consciousness of the Church, it's sure to dispel once and for all the notion that the Church is down on sex.

11. The Church should stick to religion and keep its nose out of my bedroom.

When the Church speaks about sex she *is* "sticking to religion." Sex is a religious event! According to John Paul II, when we speak of the "great sign" of the sacrament of marriage we are speaking about the entire work of creation and redemption.[13]

Sex plunges us headfirst into the Christian mystery. There's no getting around it: "Do you not know that your bodies are members of Christ?" (1 Cor 6:15).

By becoming "one flesh," spouses establish themselves and their family as the *domestic church*, a Church in miniature. Thus the Church isn't intruding into the bedroom. Christian spouses are bringing the Church into the bedroom with them.

Sex is sacred. It's holy—more so than our fallen passions sometimes wish it to be. If we think sex is somehow "better" with God out of the picture, we have it totally backward!

The joy of sex—in all its orgasmic grandeur—is meant to be the joy of loving as God loves. The joy of sex—in all its orgasmic grandeur—is meant to be a foretaste of the joys of heaven: the eternal consummation of the marriage between Christ and the Church. Christ gives us his plan for sex through the Church not to be a "kill-joy" but a "bring-joy."

"If you keep my commandments," he said, "you will abide in my love.... These things I have spoken to you, that my joy may be in you, and that your joy may be full" (Jn 15:10-11). So if you want the most awesome, joy-filled sex possible, open wide the doors to Christ—including (and especially) the bedroom door.

12. I find it quite ironic that old celibate men seek to dictate sexual morality to others. What do they know about sex?

First of all, as we clarified above, the pope and the bishops don't dictate anything to anybody. They simply witness to what God has revealed with the authority that Christ has given them. We always have the freedom to embrace it or reject it.

Second, the message they speak about sexual morality is not their own, it's God's. God created sex. He knows why he did, what it's for, how it can bring great joy when it's respected, and how it can bring great misery when it's abused. In God's wisdom (which is often so different from ours) he has entrusted his plan for sex to these "celibate old men." To repeat our earlier illustration, refusing to listen is just as foolish as putting diesel fuel in your car when the manufacturer's sticker says "unleaded gas only."

Third, anyone who doesn't think celibate men can know anything about sex has never read anything Pope John Paul II has written about it. My wife will not mind my saying that I've learned more from this "celibate old man" about the nature, beauty, and meaning of sex than from anyone else on the planet. His are the insights of a man who has plumbed the depths of his own masculine soul to make sense of his sexuality—and what he discovered there was the spark of the divine. My own life experiences—first as an unchaste teenager and young adult, and now in my own marriage—only confirm what he has to say.

Celibacy affords a desperately needed perspective. Many people have become so intoxicated by sexual indulgence that they can't see the forest for the trees. Granted, for some, forgoing genital sex for the whole of their lives may cause them to eschew their sexuality altogether (not a healthy thing, to be sure—nor is it expressive of an authentic call to the celibate vocation; see chapter nine). For others, the choice of lifelong celibacy propels them all the more to come to terms in their own soul with what sex is all about.

Pope John Paul II is a man who has clearly chosen the latter. His sacrifice of genital sex is our gain—*if* we have the courage to listen.

13. Why is the Church so obsessed with sex?

Questions like this usually refer to the Church's keen interest in upholding sexual morality. To be sure, the Church does feel an urgent need to uphold the truth about sex. Why? For all the reasons we've noted about how important the issue of sex really is.

Sexuality is not just something biological but concerns the "innermost being of the human person."[14] To the extent that our understanding of sexuality is skewed, so is our understanding of *ourselves*. Think how intertwined sex is with the mystery of life. Without sex there would be no life.

The deepest truth about sexuality actually reveals the deepest truth about life. It's this: we are called through the gift of God's grace to share in God's life by loving as he loves—and this call is stamped into our very bodies as male and female; it's stamped into our sexuality. Paraphrasing John Paul II: rediscovery of the nuptial meaning of the body always means rediscovery of the meaning of the whole of existence, the meaning of life.[15] *That's* why it's such an urgent matter.

The sexual urge taps into the most powerful drives and desires of the human heart. Depending on how they're directed, these drives and desires have the power for great good or great evil. In short, as created by God, the sexual urge was given to us as a "love instinct" that leads to life. But when it's cut off from the source of love and life (God), it tends to become a "lust instinct" that leads to death.

Sexual attitudes and behaviors, then, have the power to orient not only individuals but entire nations and societies toward respect for life—or toward its utter disregard. To be sure, when lust is woven into the fabric of a society, that society can be nothing but a "culture of death."

Sound exaggerated? Our nation alone murders over four thousand preborn babies *every day* in order to satisfy its lusts. And that's only the beginning.

Disordered sexuality is the "Pandora's box" that unleashes a host of societal evils: from the poverty of "fatherless" families and the staggering proliferation of sexually transmitted diseases (some fatal, such as AIDS), to newborns found in dumpsters and increased violence among teens—all these can be traced to the breakdown of the sexual mores that hold the family intact as the fundamental cell of society. As sexual attitudes and behaviors go, so goes marriage. As marriage goes, so goes the family. As the family goes, so goes society. Paraphrasing John Paul II once again: human life, its dignity and its balance, depends at every moment of history and at every point on the globe on the proper ordering of love between the sexes.[16]

We will never build a civilization of love and a culture of life unless we first live according to the truth of our sexuality. If the Church is "obsessed" with sex, it's because she's "obsessed" with upholding the dignity and balance of human life and the plan of God for humanity that our sexuality is meant to reveal.

Three

What Are You Saying "I Do" To?
The Basics of Marriage in the Church

There are people who try to ridicule, or even to deny, the idea of a faithful bond which lasts a lifetime. These people—you can be very sure—do not know what love is.

Pope John Paul II[1]

I'll never forget the sight of my bride processing down the aisle. She was glowing, radiant with feminine beauty. As I stood there by the altar, waiting to receive her, our eyes met and filled with tears. This was the moment. In the presence of God, the parish priest, and all our family and closest friends, we were giving our whole lives, unconditionally, to each other.

Throughout our engagement, strange as this may seem to some, there was perhaps nothing we'd discussed more than the Church's vision of marriage. We knew what the Church was holding out to us as the nature and meaning of this sacrament, and we desired it with all our hearts.

Today, in my work preparing engaged couples for marriage, I'm confronted with how few of them really understand what it is they're saying "I do" to. Marriage isn't whatever two people want it to be. For a relationship to be truly marital, it must conform to God's plan for marriage as *he* created it to be.

The questions and objections of this chapter cover "the basics" of marriage in the Church, including issues surrounding divorce and annulments and some contested Scripture passages. Since much confusion and resistance to the Church's teaching about sex stem from a misunderstanding of the meaning of marriage, this chapter will provide the necessary context for the discussion of sexual morality in the chapters that follow.

1. What exactly is marriage in the eyes of the Catholic Church?

We'll start with a basic definition paraphrasing teaching from Vatican II and canon law, and then explain each of its points:

Marriage is the intimate, exclusive, indissoluble communion of life and love entered by man and woman at the design of the Creator for the purposes of their own good and the procreation and education of children; this covenant between baptized persons has been raised by Christ the Lord to the dignity of a sacrament.[2]

Intimate communion of life and love. Marriage is the closest and most intimate of human friendships. It involves the sharing of the whole of a person's life with his or her spouse. Marriage calls for a mutual self-surrender so intimate and complete that the two spouses become "one."

Exclusive. As a mutual gift of two persons to each other, this intimate union excludes such union with anyone else. It demands the total fidelity of the spouses. This exclusivity is essential for the good of the couple's children as well.

Indissoluble. Husband and wife are not joined by passing emotion or mere erotic inclination, which, selfishly pursued, fade quickly away.[3] They're joined by God in an unbreakable bond of love through the firm and irrevocable act of their own consent. For the baptized, this bond is sealed by the Holy Spirit and, once consummated, becomes absolutely indissoluble.[4] Thus the Church does not so much teach that divorce is *wrong* but that divorce—in the sense of ending a valid marriage—is *impossible*, regardless of the civil status of a marriage.

Entered by man and woman. The complementarity of the sexes is essential to marriage. There is such widespread confusion today about the nature of marriage that some would wish to extend a legal "right" to marry to two persons of the same sex. But the very nature of marriage makes such a proposition *impossible*.

At the design of the Creator. God is the Author of marriage. He inscribed the call to marriage in our very being by creating us as male and female. Marriage is governed by his laws, faithfully transmitted by his Bride, the Church. For marriage to be what it's intended to be, it must conform to these laws. Human beings, therefore, are not free to change the meaning and purposes of marriage.

For the purposes of their own good. "It is not good that the man should be alone" (Gn 2:18). Thus, it's for their own good, for their benefit, enrichment, and ultimately their salvation, that a man and woman join their lives in the covenant of marriage. Marriage is the most basic (but not the only) expression of the vocation to love that all men and women have as persons made in God's image.

And the procreation and education of children. The fathers of Vatican II declared: "By their very nature, the institution of marriage itself and conjugal love are ordained for the procreation and education of children and find in them their ultimate crown."[5] Children are not added on to marriage and conjugal love, but spring from the very heart of the spouses' mutual self-giving, as its fruit and fulfillment. Intentional exclusion of children, then, contradicts the very nature and purpose of marriage.

Covenant. Marriage is not only a contract between a man and a woman, but a sacred covenant. God created marriage to image and participate in his own covenant with his people. Thus, the marital covenant calls spouses to share in the *free, total, faithful,* and *fruitful* love of God. Contrary to some trends in thought, the Church's recent emphasis on marriage as a covenant does not exclude the idea that marriage is also a contract. It's true that a covenant goes beyond the rights and responsibilities guaranteed by some contracts and provides a stronger, more sacred framework for marriage, but canon law still purposely uses both terms to describe marriage.[6]

The dignity of a sacrament. By virtue of their baptisms, the marriage of Christian spouses is an efficacious sign of the union between Christ and the Church, and as such is a means of grace (see the next question for a more thorough discussion). The marriage of two unbaptized persons, or of one baptized person and one unbaptized person, is considered by the Church a "good and natural" marriage.

2. What makes marriage a sacrament?

The simple answer is baptism. As John Paul II says, "Indeed, by means of baptism man and woman are definitively placed within ... the spousal covenant of Christ and the Church. And it is because of this indestructible insertion that [marriage] is elevated and assumed into the spousal charity of Christ, sustained and enriched by his redeeming power."[7]

Still, of all the seven sacraments (baptism, confirmation, Eucharist, reconciliation, anointing of the sick, holy orders, and marriage), marriage seems, at first glance, the most unlike a sacrament. Marriage isn't unique to Christians, after all, but it's common to all cultures and all religions. So what makes such an "earthy" reality as marriage a sacrament? To provide a more thorough answer to this question, we first need to understand better what sacraments are.

If you had religion classes in your childhood, you may remember being taught that a sacrament is "an outward sign instituted by Christ to give grace."[8] For most people this textbook definition fails to capture how wonderful and profound the sacraments really are. Through these "visible signs instituted by Christ" we actually encounter the *eternal* God in the *temporal* world and become sharers in his divine life.

An infinite abyss separates Creator and creature. The wonder of the sacraments is that they bridge this infinite gap. Sacraments are where heaven and earth "kiss," where God and humanity become one *in the flesh.*

God is invisible. Sacraments allow us to see him under the veil of visible things. God is intangible. Sacraments allow us to touch him. God is incommunicable. Sacraments are our communion with him.

This communion of God and humanity is a living reality in the person of Jesus Christ. Thus the sacramental life of the Church flows directly from the dynamism of the Incarnation, the mystery of the Word made flesh, God made Man. In Christ, God has forever wed himself to our flesh and impregnated the material world with his saving power. Indeed, as Tertullian, an early Church Father, declared: "The flesh has become the hinge of salvation."[9]

In contrast to authentic sacramental spirituality, there is a widespread but gravely mistaken notion of spirituality that tends to devalue the body, view it with suspicion, or at times even treat it with contempt. Catholicism, far from devaluing the body, is a deeply *sensual* religion. That's to say, it's in and through *the body* (sensually) that we encounter the divine.

God doesn't communicate himself to us by some sort of spiritual osmosis. Rather he meets us where we are as earthly, bodily creatures. This is the great gift of the sacraments.

We truly become sharers in divine life through bathing *the body* with water (baptism); through anointing *the body* with oil and the laying on of *hands* (Confirmation, holy orders, anointing of the sick); through confessing with our *lips* and receiving the *spoken* words of absolution (reconciliation); through *eating* and *drinking* the *Body* and *Blood* of Christ (Eucharist); and yes, through the encounter that makes a man and woman "one *flesh*" (marriage).

Did I just imply that the marital embrace is an encounter with Christ and a sharing in divine life? Yes, I did. Through intercourse, the spouses *enact* their sacrament. It's where the words of the wedding vows become flesh, and, as such, it's the visible sign of the sacrament of marriage. As Pope John Paul II says: "The sacrament, as a visible sign, is constituted with Man, as a body, by means of his visible masculinity and femininity. The body, in fact, and it alone, is capable of making visible what is invisible; the spiritual and the divine. It was created to transfer into the visible reality of the world the mystery hidden since time immemorial in God, and thus be a sign of it."[10]

Plain English, please. The pope is saying here that God created our bodies as male and female to be a sign in the world that reveals his own eternal mystery, and this happens most specifically when husband and wife unite their bodies in "one flesh."[11] What is this mystery hidden in God from all eternity? In a nutshell (as if it were possible to put God in a nutshell), it's God's trinitarian life and his amazing plan for us to share in this life through Christ as members of the Church. *This* is what marriage symbolizes and reveals.

Sacraments are *efficacious* signs, which means they truly communicate what they symbolize. So the love of husband and wife is not merely a symbol of the love of Christ and the Church. For the baptized, it's a *real* participation in it. This is a "profound mystery," as St. Paul says (or as some translations say, this is a "great sacrament"—see Eph 5:32).

Because all the sacraments are meant to draw us more deeply into the marriage of Christ and the Church, John Paul II calls marriage the "prototype" of all the sacraments.[12] He even goes so far as to say that inasmuch as the visible sign of marriage (the marital embrace) is linked to the visible sign of Christ and the Church (the Eucharist), it transfers God's eternal plan of love into history, making it "the foundation of the whole sacramental order."[13]

Translation: The "one flesh" union of husband and wife is the fundamental revelation in the created world of the eternal mystery of God, inasmuch as it points us to the greatest of all sacraments, the "one flesh" union of Christ and the Church in the Eucharist. Wow! Marriage is the foundation of *all* the outward signs instituted by Christ to give grace. *This* is what makes marriage a sacrament.

3. The Church's teaching against divorce leaves some women in abusive relationships with no escape.

In the case of an abusive relationship, the Church readily recognizes the need of spouses to separate and even, if necessary, obtain a civil divorce. Still, such a decree would not *end* a valid marriage. Death alone ends marriage.

4. If the Church believes marriage is "until death do you part," why are there so many annulments?

There's a great deal of confusion today about annulments. An annulment (properly referred to as a "declaration of nullity") is not a "Catholic version of divorce." A divorce declares that you were once married but now you are no longer. A declaration of nullity is an official statement by the Church that a valid marriage *never existed in the first place.*

The Church is consistent with her own teaching on the permanence of marriage and in granting declarations of nullity. Valid, consummated, sacramental marriages can never be dissolved under any circumstance. But if it turns out that, despite all appearances, a couple was never validly married, then their relationship has no binding force.

Why are so many annulments granted today? It's not outside the realm of possibility that at times the system is abused. On the other hand, the number of annulments granted today may well be an accurate reflection of the number of couples who do not enter marriage validly. First of all, tribunals in the United States report that one-fourth to one-third of all annulments granted are due to "lack of form." This means large numbers of baptized Catholics are getting married *outside the Catholic Church.* If they do this without a dispensation, their marriage is null from the start (see next question).

Furthermore, people born in the latter half of the twentieth century have been raised in a culture that not only has lost a support structure for marriage but also very loudly, incessantly, and convincingly promotes values that are *antithetical* to marriage. The effects of this culture on people's ability to enter marriage validly cannot be underestimated.

5. What makes a marriage valid?

Marriage is brought about by the legitimately manifested consent (vows) of a properly qualified bride and groom. Among other things, this means that the bride and groom are the ministers of the sacrament of marriage. Although people typically say Fr. so-and-so married us, that's incorrect. Fr. so-and-so hasn't married anybody—he's a celibate. The priest (or deacon) only serves as an official witness for the Church.[14]

This is an important point. Marriage is not something that simply "happens" to the couple by virtue of wearing a white dress and a tuxedo and going through the motions of a wedding ceremony. Marriage only "happens" if bride and groom minister it to each other.

If they don't, they aren't married, even if they went through the motions. Of course, if a Catholic couple has had a wedding ceremony in accordance with the teaching of the Church, we're always to assume they did minister the sacrament to each other. The Church always assumes the validity of a marriage unless proven otherwise.

But back to the question: What makes a marriage valid? Providing a comprehensive response is the task of an entire book, and several of those have been written.[15] It's only possible to provide a general overview here.

In order for the marriage of Catholics to be validly established, spouses must: (1) not have any impediments to marriage; (2) follow the proper form of the sacrament; (3) have the proper capacity to exchange consent and do so freely and unconditionally; and (4) consent to what the Church intends by marriage, that is: *fidelity*, *indissolubility*, and *openness to children*. Let's look at each of these aspects individually.

Spouses must not have any impediments to marriage. Impediments are prohibitions to marriage originating from divine or natural law and Church law. There are twelve:[16]

- *Age.* A man under age 16, and a woman under age 14, cannot marry validly. (Keep in mind we're dealing with a universal Church. While marrying at these ages wouldn't be recommended in most developed countries, in some cultures it's common.)
- *Impotence.* Definitive and perpetual inability to have intercourse.
- *Previous bond.* Preexistence of a valid marriage to someone else.
- *Disparity of cult.* When a baptized Catholic attempts to marry an unbaptized person (though a dispensation from this impediment can be granted in certain cases).
- *Sacred orders.* Persons bound by holy orders—that is, deacons,[17] priests, and bishops—cannot marry.
- *Perpetual vows of chastity.* Public vows of chastity taken in a religious institute (that is, an institute of religious brothers or sisters).
- *Abduction.* When a person has been abducted for the purpose of marriage.
- *Crime.* When a previous spouse has been murdered in order to "free" someone to marry.
- *Consanguinity.* Blood relationships including anyone closer than second cousins.
- *Affinity.* In-law relationships in the direct line. (For example, a stepfather could not marry his stepdaughter, but a man could marry his deceased wife's sister.)

- *Public propriety.* When an unmarried person cohabiting with someone else wishes to enter marriage with a close relative in the direct line of the person with whom he or she has been living. (For example, a woman living with a man cannot marry either his father or his son.)
- *Adoption.* Family relationships established by adoption to the degree mentioned above.

Spouses must follow the proper form of the sacrament.[18] This requires the presence of an official witness (usually a priest or deacon) who receives their consent in the name of the Church and two other witnesses (usually the "best man" and the "maid or matron of honor"), who are also present for the exchange of vows. Thus baptized Catholics who marry outside the Church (for example, in a civil ceremony or in another denomination) do so invalidly. If a Catholic wishes to marry a non-Catholic and has sufficient reason to hold the ceremony in a non-Catholic setting, a dispensation from the form can be granted.

Spouses must have the capacity to exchange consent and do so freely and unconditionally.[19] A person must be psychologically capable of understanding what the marriage commitment entails and must be capable of committing to it. Thus serious maladies of a psychological nature can invalidate a person's consent. Further, if consent is offered under fear or duress it is not valid. Thus there is no such thing as a "shotgun wedding." Nor can couples place *any* conditions on their consent—that is, they can't be thinking, "I'll only stay married *if* ... " Consent must assume that "come what may, we are married forever."

Spouses must consent to what the Church intends by marriage, that is, fidelity, indissolubility, and openness to children. It is essentially to these three promises that bride and groom say "I do." These promises are so much a part of what marriage *is* that if either bride or groom withholds consent to any of them, they are not truly married.

6. What does it mean to withhold consent from these promises?

Withholding consent involves a concrete act of the will that's contrary to any of these promises. It means that at the time of consent, when the person's lips said "I do," his or her will said "I don't." This is to be distinguished from butterflies, questions, and even minor doubts. These are normal enough and don't necessarily call into question the sincerity of a person's consent. A closer look at each of these promises will help us understand to what couples must consent.

Fidelity. Marriage by its very nature demands faithfulness of heart, mind, and action to your one and only spouse. If bride and groom don't commit themselves to such fidelity, they are not committing to marriage. There is no such thing as an "open marriage," for example. The very term is self-contradictory. It's important to clarify, however, that subsequent failings in this area do not, in themselves, invalidate a marriage, so long as both spouses sincerely committed to fidelity at the time of consent.

Indissolubility. Marriage establishes an unbreakable, lifelong bond between the spouses. If this isn't what bride and groom intend to establish, then they don't intend to establish a marriage. Marriage is all or nothing. This means there's no such thing as a "trial marriage," in which a man and a woman "just see" if it works out. Like "open marriage," the very term is self-contradictory. Once a valid marriage has been consummated, the bond that God establishes between the spouses can be broken only by death.

Openness to children. Children flow directly from the very nature of married love to such a degree that if a couple has absolutely no intention of having children and *positively* excludes them from their relationship, then their relationship is not one of marriage. The "child-free by choice marriage," becoming more popular today, is also self-contradictory.

7. What if a couple just doesn't think they'd make good parents? Are you saying the Church won't let them get married?

It's not that the Church won't "let" them get married. It's that such a couple doesn't actually *want* to get married. They want to have a sexual relationship that intentionally excludes children, and it's assumed they will do so by intentionally sterilizing their acts of intercourse. Whatever kind of relationship this is, it's *not* marriage.

Marriage, as part of its definition, is a sexual relationship in which spouses are open to the possibility that God may bless them with children. Spouses commit themselves never *intentionally* to sterilize their acts of intercourse. If a couple refuses ever to engage in noncontracepted intercourse (that is, an act of intercourse that's open to children), then they don't want to commit to marriage. This is how an intention against the good of children is to be understood.

If we truly understand what the marriage commitment *is*, then people who don't think they would make good parents must also admit they would not make good spouses. The self-sacrificial love that's necessary to be a good mother or father is the same kind of love that's necessary to be a good husband or wife. This is sometimes difficult to understand for people raised in developed countries. The widespread "contraceptive mentality" has afforded members of our culture the illusion that children are a superfluous, optional "add-on" to a sexually active relationship. But such a mentality is utterly incompatible with a Catholic faith perspective.

8. What if a couple is unable to have children?

Marriage retains its intrinsic goodness even without children, so long as they're not positively excluded. Thus, unintended infertility is *not* an impediment to marriage.

This condition is often confused with the impediment of impotence. Impotence isn't an impediment to marriage because such a couple can't have children. It's an impediment because they can't have intercourse. Whether a child *does* or *does not* come from intercourse is up to God. If *he* chooses not to bring a child forth from the spouses' union, their marriage is no less valid because of it.

9. I can't believe how unfeeling it is for the Church to withhold the sacrament of marriage from people who are impotent. Sex isn't everything in marriage.

Of all the impediments to marriage, this is the one that seems to trouble people the most. So it's worth taking some time to explain.

No, sex isn't everything in marriage. But it's so essential to what marriage *is* that if there's absolutely no possibility of intercourse ever happening, there's no possibility of marriage ever happening. To clarify, it has to be *definitive* and *perpetual* impotence. This, we must realize, is extremely rare.

It's important not to let our sympathies cloud sound reasoning. For example, when people learn about this impediment, they'll often think of the sufferings of veterans wounded in war who can't function sexually. Indeed, this is a sad situation that's worthy of our sympathy.

But it doesn't change the objective truth of the matter. Sympathy for the blind, for example, shouldn't lead the state to issue blind people driver's licenses. It's a sad situation, but blind people *can't* do what driving requires. Similarly, definitively impotent people can't do what marriage requires. Jesus himself confirms this when he speaks of the inability of "eunuchs" (people unable to have sex) to marry (see Mt 19:12).

This impediment isn't unreasonable but is actually very sensible. Think about it. What is it that a man and a woman pledge to share with one another that makes their relationship one of marriage rather than, say, just a nice friendship? What is it that a husband and a wife share with one another that is so unique and intrinsic to *their* relationship that it would be a violation of the very meaning of marriage to share it with someone else?

What exactly is it that makes marriage an "intimate, exclusive, indissoluble joining of man and woman's lives for their own good and the procreation and education of children"? Sexual intercourse. Sexual intercourse is the defining element of marital love. This doesn't mean marriage can be reduced *merely* to sexual intercourse (no more than driving a car can be reduced *merely* to seeing). But dispense with its possibility, and you no longer have marriage.

We must recognize the influence of the prevailing culture in the difficulty that people have with this impediment. The sexual revolution loosed sex from its social and psychological moorings. Thus for the typical modern mind, sex no longer expresses the marriage commitment. It just expresses some vague sort of desire for pleasure and intimacy, or worse, just a desire for selfish gratification.

The assumptions here are faulty: Sure, married people have sex, but so do lots of other people, and there's nothing wrong with that, right? So, if a couple couldn't have sex for some reason, what bearing would that have on their desire to get married? From the perspective of the modern mind-set, none. But from the perspective of the true meaning of sex, it would have direct bearing, so much so that marriage would be *impossible*.

Here's a silly analogy that may help clarify things. You can't reduce chocolate chip cookies merely to chocolate chips, but without the chocolate chips, you no longer have chocolate chip cookies. Chocolate chips are what define this type of cookie. There are other kinds of cookies, but if they don't have chocolate chips, they can't honestly be called chocolate chip cookies.

Similarly, without the *possibility* of sexual intercourse, you can't honestly call the love that a man and woman share "marriage." It doesn't mean they're incapable of love. It just means they're incapable of that unique kind of love called *marital* love.

There are many kinds of love, just like there are many kinds of cookies. Two people may very much want to make chocolate chip cookies, but if by some misfortune they have no possibility of acquiring chocolate chips, the plain reality is they're unable to make chocolate chip cookies. They'll have to make some other kind of cookies.

To go further with this banal analogy: If by some tragedy a couple is definitively and perpetually unable to express the defining element of marriage, then the reality is that their love (while it may be a very beautiful, lasting, and intimate love) cannot be the unique and specific love that makes a marriage. No amount of sentiment or sympathy for individual situations—as understandable as such feelings are—can change this reality.

10. Marriage is just as much a spiritual union as a physical one. So what if you can't have sex?

This is certainly true, but the two realities (physical and spiritual) cannot be separated. To do so is actually to fall into an age-old heresy in the Church known as *dualism*. Dualism makes a divorce in human nature between what is physical and what is spiritual. But human beings are an indivisible marriage of flesh and spirit, body and soul. We're not persons "in" a body that can be dispensed with. We're *body-persons*. This means that our spiritual reality as human beings is expressed through our bodies as male and female.

The spiritual and physical principles in us are so united that only death can separate them. And even after death, the soul is in an unnatural state until it's reunited with the body in the resurrection at the second coming of Christ. Only then will the souls in heaven become, once again, *fully human* as body-persons (just as Christ and his Blessed Mother are now in heaven body and soul).

Because of this profound spiritual and physical unity of the human person, it's incorrect, strictly speaking, to make a sharp distinction between "physical" and "spiritual" love in human beings. What we do with our bodies we do with our souls, and what we do with our souls we can only do through our existence as body-persons. Human love is manifested through the human body.

Emotions themselves (not that we can reduce love to mere emotion) are communicated through the body. We can't even pray without the body. As Pope John Paul II says, any attempt to break the personal unity of soul and body "strikes at God's creation itself at the level of the deepest interaction of nature and person."[20]

This profound spiritual and physical unity in humanity is the very principle of the Church's sacramental life—including the sacrament of marriage. For even God, who is pure Spirit, in order to show human beings his love, took on a body: "And the Word became flesh" (Jn 1:14). *All* sacraments are *bodily*, *physical* realities.

It's in and through their bodies that husband and wife express the love that's unique to the sacrament of marriage. Their "one flesh" union (or at least its possibility) is no more dispensable to the sacrament of marriage than bread and wine are to the Eucharist or water is to baptism. It's in and through these physical realities that the spiritual realities proper to each of these sacraments are communicated. Without the physical reality of the sacrament, there simply is no sacrament.

11. My parents were married for more than twenty-five years, with five kids, but even they were granted an annulment by the Church. How can the Church all of a sudden say after so much time that my parents' marriage never existed? Doesn't this make me an "illegitimate child"?

First, a clarification about "legitimacy." This is a term used by various legal systems throughout the world to ensure a child's paternity. (It's usually quite obvious who the mother is.) From a faith perspective, however, God is the Father of us all. So, regardless of the circumstances of conception, there is really no such thing as an "illegitimate child" in God's eyes.

An annulment, then, does *not* make the children of that relationship illegitimate. This is a common misunderstanding that needs unambiguous clarification. Furthermore, a declaration of nullity from the Church does not affect the state's legal recognition of the paternity of the children. Even legally speaking, the children remain "legitimate."

A declaration of nullity does not and cannot erase your parents' relationship. They obviously were together for many years. They had good times and bad. They conceived and raised children. None of this is "wiped away." It's certainly difficult to come to terms with the fact that on the day of the wedding, something prevented your parents from entering marriage validly. But, again, it's important not to let sentiment cloud sound reasoning.

Sound reasoning recognizes that marriage is not something that just "happens" to a couple by going through the motions of a wedding. Some things— many things—can prevent couples from entering marriage validly. While most invalid marriages are determined to be such within the early years of the relationship, it's not impossible for a couple to live together for many years and raise a family, only later to discover after a thorough tribunal investigation that their marriage was not entered validly.

Children of marriages that have been declared null by the Church should never despair. It's God's very nature to bring good out of all situations. In fact, such children are perhaps the greatest good that God brings out of marriages that are later proven invalid.

12. My sister (a Catholic) wants to marry a Protestant who is divorced, but her priest said he would need to apply for an annulment, and if he didn't get one, they couldn't get married. Why does the Church make even Protestants go through the annulment process?

Since only Catholics are bound to observe the Catholic form of marriage, the Church recognizes the marriages of all non-Catholics and assumes they are valid unions unless proven otherwise. She even recognizes the marriage of two baptized Protestants as a sacrament, even if they themselves don't believe marriage is a sacrament and even if the wedding took place in the presence of a justice of the peace. Thus your sister can't marry a man who is already validly married to someone else.

According to Christ's own words, that would be committing adultery (see Lk 16:18). Civil divorce never changes one's actual marital status in the eyes of the Church, whether Catholic or not.

If they would like to pursue the matter, however, he is free to apply for a declaration of nullity to see whether his first marriage was valid. (Close to 20 percent of annulment cases actually deal with non-Catholics.) If it's determined that it wasn't valid, your sister would then be free to marry him.

But keep in mind, annulments are never a sure thing. It has to be proven with moral certainty that on the day of the wedding some defect prevented the couple from entering marriage validly. It would be wrong for your sister even to consider marriage unless and until an annulment were granted.

13. Why doesn't the Church get with the times and admit that some marriages just don't work out?

It's obvious to everyone, including the Church, that some marriages "don't work out." As mentioned earlier, in serious circumstances the Church even encourages separation of "bed and board." But this is very different from accepting divorce.

It's hard to overestimate the importance that the Church places on defending the permanence of marriage. History tells the tale of entire nations separating from the Catholic Church because of disputes over this point.

Why is the Church so obstinate? Because marriage is where human and divine love "kiss." To diminish in any way the permanence of married love is to diminish the permanence of God's love. As a sacrament, marriage is a true participation in the love of Christ for his Bride, the Church.

If we truly understand this, to admit divorce is to say in the same breath that Christ has left the Church. *Impossible!* Christ will never, ever abandon his Bride. This is what's at stake.

But we're not God, people say. How can we love as Christ loves?

On our own we cannot. But "with God all things are possible" (Mt 19:26). It's no coincidence that these words of Christ from the Gospel of Matthew appear shortly after Christ's teaching on the permanence of marriage (see Mt 19:1-11). When Christ's disciples learned what the permanence of marriage demanded of them, they thought it would be better not to marry at all (see Mt 19:10). Jesus responded, "Not all men can receive this precept, but only those to whom it is given" (Mt 19:11).

To whom is this teaching on the permanence of marriage given? To men and women who remain slaves to their weaknesses? No! To men and women who have been given the power to love as Christ loves through the Holy Spirit!

This is the good news of the gospel. Christ's love has been poured into our hearts through the Holy Spirit (see Rom 5:5). This means husbands and wives *can* love one another as Christ loves.

What's at stake in the permanence of marriage is really a question of faith. Do we believe in the good news of the gospel, or don't we? Do we believe it's possible to love one another as Christ loves, or don't we?

To admit the possibility of divorce is to say that Christ cannot save us from our sin. Woe to the Church if she were ever to say such a thing. The permanence of marriage is an objective reality to which the Church must bear witness if she is to tell the truth.

14. Didn't even Jesus say divorce was acceptable in the case of adultery?

This is commonly referred to as the "exception clause." It appears in Matthew 5:32 and 19:9, where Jesus prohibits divorce except in the case of *porneia*. This Greek word is sometimes translated as "unchastity," "impurity," "lewd conduct," or—less accurately—"adultery." Many biblical scholars believe the exception clause refers to marriages that were not true marriages because they were within the forbidden degrees of blood relationship (see Lv 18:6-16). Thus it would be expected that Christians who found themselves in these incestuous relationships would "divorce."

The exception clause does not appear in the parallel passages of Luke 16:18 or Mark 10:11-12. First Corinthians 7:10-11 also expresses the prohibition against divorce as an unconditional command from the Lord for his followers. This is the way the Church, as the authority that Christ instituted to speak on such matters, has always understood it.

It simply would make no sense for Christ to teach that people could divorce if one or the other spouse committed adultery. All one would need do, then, if he wanted a divorce, would be to go out and cheat on his spouse. The commonly held interpretation of *porneia* is much more plausible.

15. My brother is a good Catholic who loves his new wife and loves God. But because he wasn't granted an annulment of his first marriage, he can't receive Communion. He feels left out and unappreciated by the Church. Why is the Catholic Church so harsh and insensitive about these things? Other churches welcome people no matter what.

Christ's love is welcoming of all. If the Church fails to show her members the love of Christ, she has failed indeed. So, too, we must admit, if the Church fails to challenge her members to live the love of Christ, she has failed indeed.

There's a certain tension here. Christ's love is unconditionally welcoming of sinners, but in his love for us he is uncompromising with our sin. As with the woman caught in adultery, he does not condemn us. But he calls us to sin no more (see Jn 8:10-11).

Welcoming a person can never mean welcoming that person's objectively wrong choices. Christ said, "Whoever divorces his wife and marries another, commits adultery against her" (Mk 10:11). Thus, if your brother's ("first") marriage was valid, by living in a sexually active relationship with someone else, he's actually committing adultery against his ("first") wife.

Christ, our heavenly Bridegroom, shows us what sexual union means by making an everlasting gift of his body to us (his Bride) on the cross, which we receive sacramentally in the Eucharist. The sexual union of husband and wife participates in Christ's Eucharistic self-giving. Yet the sexual union of two people who aren't married is a direct contradiction of the Eucharistic love of Christ. This is even more so when one or both of the sexual partners is married to someone else.

For this reason, a Catholic person who persists in engaging in intercourse with someone, when in reality he or she is married to someone else, is not able to receive Communion. Objectively speaking, such a person is living in direct contradiction to what the Eucharist means. In the Eucharist, we consummate our marriage with Christ. In it, Christ gives himself to us completely, and we give ourselves to him completely, pledging total faithfulness to him. If we don't intend to be faithful to Christ's teachings, then it would be hypocritical to receive the Eucharist.

It's very important to distinguish here between willfully persisting in an objective "state of sin" and struggling with resisting sin. Being faithful to Christ is difficult. For every human being it's a struggle.

By no means is the Eucharist only for those who are "perfect." If that were the case, no one could go to Communion. But at the very least, in receiving the Eucharist we are telling Christ that we're willing to struggle to live according to his will, resisting all that is contrary to it.

Will we fail at times? Certainly. Such is the fallen human condition. And that's why Christ graciously provides us with the sacrament of reconciliation.

16. Every time I hear that Scripture verse that says, "Wives, be subject to your husbands," the hair stands up on the back of my neck. Why should I listen to what the Bible says about marriage when it's so demeaning toward women?

The verse you're referring to is Ephesians 5:22. If it makes the hair on the back of your neck stand up, I want to affirm your response. Why? Because you probably think the passage means something like: "Wives are doormats who must surrender to their husbands' domination." If that's what you think it means, then I'd be concerned if it didn't make the hair on the back of your neck stand up.

Nevertheless, that's *not* what the verse means. When we look at this verse in the context of the whole passage (Eph 5:21-33), the context flips the typical interpretation on its head. Unfortunately, as soon as people hear this one verse, they tune out the rest of what St. Paul says.

While we must admit that some men throughout history have pointed to this Scripture verse to justify their fallen desire to dominate women, St. Paul is in no way justifying such an attitude. He knows it to be a result of sin (see Gn 3:16), which is why in this passage he's actually restoring God's original plan before sin. He does so by pointing out what marriage was all about in the first place. It was meant to foreshadow the marriage of Christ and the Church. St. Paul simply draws out the implications of this analogy.

He starts by calling both husbands and wives to *be subject to one another* "out of reverence for Christ" (v. 21)—out of reverence for the "great mystery" that spouses participate in by imaging Christ's union with the Church. In the analogy, the husband represents Christ, and the wife represents the Church. So, he says, as the Church is subject to Christ, so should wives also be subject to their husbands (see v. 24).

Another translation uses the word "submission." I like to explain this word as follows. "Sub" means "under," and "mission" means "to be sent forth with the authority to perform a specific service." Wives, then, are called to put themselves "under" the "mission" of their husbands.

What's the mission of the husband? "Husbands, love your wives, as Christ loved the Church and gave himself up for her" (v. 25). How did Christ love the Church? He died for her. Christ said he came "not to be served but to serve," and to lay down his life for his Bride (Mt 20:28).

What, then, does it mean for a wife to "submit" to her husband? It means let your husband serve you. Put yourself under his mission to love you as Christ loved the Church. As John Paul II says: "The wife's 'submission' to her husband, understood in the context of the entire passage of the letter to the Ephesians, signifies above all the 'experiencing of love.' This is true all the more so since this 'submission' is related to the image of the submission of the Church to Christ, which certainly consists in experiencing his love."[21]

What woman would not want to receive this kind of love from her husband? What woman would not want to be subject to her husband if he truly took his mission seriously to love her as Christ loved the Church? So often it's husbands that want their wives to take this Scripture passage to heart. I think it's we men who need to take it to heart first.

17. Didn't Jesus say there's no marriage after the resurrection? Why not? Does this mean my wife and I won't be together in heaven?

In chapter 22 of the Gospel of Matthew (see also Mk 12 and Lk 20), the Sadducees, a group of Jews who didn't believe in the resurrection of the dead, came to Jesus with a scenario that they thought would corner him into denying the resurrection as well. A man had a wife, and he died. One of his brothers married her to give his deceased brother offspring, but he died too. This happened again and again until seven brothers had all been married to the same woman in succession. The Sadducees then asked Christ whose wife she would be in the resurrection.

Christ responded, "You are wrong, because you know neither the scriptures nor the power of God. For in the resurrection, they neither marry nor are given in marriage" (vv. 29-30).

For many this saying of Christ strikes a sour note. Why? Because we know neither the Scriptures nor the power of God. If we did, we would rejoice in these words. Christ's statement is not a devaluation of marriage; rather, it points to the ultimate purpose and meaning of this wonderful sacrament.

Marriage in this life is meant to point us to heaven, where, for all eternity, we will celebrate the "marriage of the Lamb" (Rv 19:7), the marriage of Christ and the Church. This is the deepest desire of the human heart—to live in the eternal bliss of marital intimacy with God himself. As wonderful as marriage can be in this life, it's only a sign, a foretaste, a *sacrament* of this joy to come. Earthly marriage is simply preparation for heavenly marriage.

It's the same with all the sacraments. They prepare us for heaven. There are no sacraments in heaven, because they all will have come to fruition. Human beings will no longer need signs to point them *to* heaven when they are *in* heaven.

Think of it in terms of road signs. If your destination is Denver, Colorado, then once you arrive you no longer need a sign to point you there.

Will you be with your spouse in heaven? Of course, if you both accept Christ's marriage proposal and live in fidelity to him in this life. In fact, every member of the human race who accepts the invitation to the heavenly wedding feast will be in the most intimate possible communion with everyone else.

This is what we call the "communion of saints." In heaven, all that separates and divides us on earth will be done away with. We'll all live in a heavenly *communion of persons* as the one Bride of Christ. And as the one **Bride** of Christ, we'll live in the ecstatic (dare I say heavenly orgasmic?) bliss of **consummated** union with our Bridegroom, Christ the Lord. We will *know* God and see him as he is, face to face (see 1 Cor 13:12).

Four

What to Do Before "I Do"

Chastity Outside of Marriage

The person who does not decide to love forever will find it very difficult to really love for even one day.

Pope John Paul II[1]

Now it's time to address some of the "nitty-gritties" of sexual morality. While this chapter will focus on the questions and objections of unmarried people, we'll also address various themes that are just as pertinent to those who are married. So if you're hitched, don't just skip to the next chapter—there's something here for you as well.

Speaking of "do's" and "don'ts" is unavoidable in any discussion about morality. But it's important not to misconstrue such discussion as a *minimalist* approach to following Christ. We shouldn't be seeking how much we can "get away with" before being guilty of doing something wrong.

If this is our perspective, we'll be unable to see the Church's teaching as the good news that it is. Instead, we'll view it with suspicion. We'll see it as an arbitrary moral code that bans the things we *really* want to do. We'll see Church teaching as a burden imposed from outside that's difficult, if not impossible, to live up to. This sentiment is virtually inevitable unless we encounter the person of Christ in a life-transforming way.

The person whose heart has been transformed by Christ is not seeking to "get away" with anything. Such a person is instead always seeking what it means to follow Christ as the model of love and self-giving. He doesn't see the Church's teaching as an imposition, but recognizes it for what it is—the truth about love that God has written in our very being.

When Christ is desired for who he is, his Church's teachings aren't viewed with suspicion or seen as something to *live up to*. Rather, they're trusted as the standard never to *fall below* if one is seeking true love, true joy, true fulfillment. In that light, we should approach these important issues with a prayer:

Lord Jesus, help me to see that the moral teachings of your Church are not impersonal and imposed standards of an arbitrary moral code, but are truly your own design written in my heart as a man (woman) through which I discover the meaning of life and love. Soften my heart to receive and live the truth that sets me free. Amen.

1. What does chastity mean?

Admittedly, the word "chastity" itself tends to have negative connotations and is in need of rehabilitation. For many it's synonymous with a repressive "just don't do it" approach to sex. But chastity is actually a positive virtue, because it orders our sexual desires, thoughts, and behaviors toward the truth of authentic love.

Chastity is not primarily a *no* to illicit sex. Chastity is first and foremost a great *yes* to the true meaning of sex, to the goodness of being created as male and female in the image of God. Chastity isn't repressive. It's totally liberating. It frees us from the tendency to use others for selfish gratification and enables us to love others as Christ loves us. The virtue of chastity is therefore essential if we are to discover and fulfill the very meaning of our being and existence.

2. Why shouldn't two consenting adults who love each other be able to have sex? What difference does a marriage certificate really make, anyway?

Two unmarried consenting adults are *able* to have sex. The question is this: Is it *good* for them to do so? What are unmarried people saying to each other by having sex? Is it in keeping with the true meaning of sex? Is it loving?

Love is not arbitrary. Love is not whatever I want it to be. Love is not simply warm gooey feelings for another person. Love can't simply be equated with sexual attraction toward, nor sexual desire for, another person. Love is not something that "happens" to people. Love is a decision.

I don't say this to downplay the role of emotions and attractions. As John Paul II says, these are the "raw material" of love. But it's a mistake to regard the raw material as the "finished form."[2] A person must allow grace to shape and form the raw material into a free choice for the good of the beloved. Of course, this concept is foreign to our popular culture. A scene from the Robert Redford movie *The Horse Whisperer* illustrates what I mean.

When a stressed-out, unhappily married city woman realizes she has "fallen in love" with a laid-back, divorced cowboy, she declares, "I didn't want this to happen." Proof-positive that whatever feelings she had for said cowboy weren't feelings of love.

By definition, love always *chooses freely* to sacrifice oneself for the good of the beloved. Sexual love chooses freely to make a total, faithful, and fruitful gift of self to the beloved. Sexual intercourse speaks this language—the language of God's love. This is the language of the marriage bond, the language of wedding vows. Anything less is a cheap counterfeit for what our hearts truly desire.

Language is meant to convey truth. It's an abuse of language to convey lies, and it can never be loving to do so. The "language" of the body is also meant to convey truth. John Paul II actually speaks of the "prophetism of the body." The body is a "prophet" because it speaks the language of God, which is love.

But we must be careful to distinguish between true and false prophets.[3] Two "consenting adults" who are having sex but haven't made the marriage commitment are "false prophets." They're saying something with their bodies: "I am yours freely, totally, faithfully, fruitfully, forever." But in fact, what they say isn't true. They're lying to one another.

Two consenting adults who *truly* love one another and want to express that love through sexual intercourse are two adults who want to consent to marriage. Out of their love for each other, and out of their desire never to speak dishonestly to each other, they won't speak the "language" of their bodies through intercourse until that language is an expression of the commitment they have *already made* in their wedding vows.

So what difference does a marriage certificate make? In itself, not much. It's just a piece of paper. But such a piece of paper indicates that God has established the marriage bond between the spouses. And that bond makes every difference in the world.

When a bride and groom stand at the altar and declare their consent before the Church, it's not merely a formal recognition of something that already exists between them. At the moment they give their consent, bride and groom are fundamentally changed. They *become* right then and there (and only right then and there) *husband* and *wife*. What did not exist five minutes before does exist now—a marital bond sealed by the Holy Spirit that, once consummated, can never be dissolved by anything but death.

Sexual intercourse is the expression of *this* bond. It's the visible sign of this invisible reality. If this bond doesn't exist between a man and a woman, sexual intercourse between them is utterly void of its *raison d'être*.

Regardless of how much passion, feeling, and sentiment may be involved, such acts of intercourse can never be acts of true love. If the couple understand what sex and marriage mean, and live out of respect for that meaning, then the thought that they would have sex before God establishes the marriage bond between them (via their consent) is *unthinkable*.[4]

A couple who is regularly engaging in sex before they marry, and sees nothing wrong with it, demonstrates that they don't understanding the meaning of sex and marriage. Such a couple will most likely fail to comprehend the significance of the marriage bond altogether. They'll tend to reduce the change in their relationship to a piece of paper—a "marriage certificate"—and continue having sex as they always did.

The fact that the couple is now married does not automatically make their sexual union what it's supposed to be. Sex is only what it's supposed to be if it expresses the commitment to free, total, faithful, and fruitful self-giving. There are many married couples who have plenty of sex that actually violates their own wedding vows. The fact that it's happening after the wedding has taken place doesn't make it OK.

Instead of framing the discussion in terms of *premarital* sex versus *postmarital* sex, it's much more accurate to speak of *nonmarital* sex versus *marital* sex. It's impossible for unmarried people to have marital sex. They have no marriage bond to express, no wedding vows to renew. On the other hand, while the existence of a marriage bond is no *guarantee* that sex will always be marital, it is an absolute prerequisite for the possibility.

3. I went to Catholic schools for twelve years and never heard this. Why not?

This is a typical response to lectures I give across the country. The answer's complex, but the simple version is that many of the Church's educators have themselves been duped to one degree or another by the prevailing mentality. It's fairly common for teachers who openly dissent from Church teaching to hold prominent positions in Catholic seminaries, colleges, and universities. The same problem exists in many Catholic high schools, grade schools, and parish-based religious education programs.

It's not an alarmist claim to say that there is a crisis within Catholic education. In response to this crisis, God has blessed the Church with a pope who has done more to uphold and explain the Church's teaching on sex than any other pope in history. John Paul II has brought to the Church a vision never before articulated about the dignity and meaning of the human body and of sexual union. Although it may seem as if few are listening, I believe we're on the verge of a new sexual revolution, and that it's only a matter of time before his revolutionary insights become part of the fabric of the Catholic community, and indeed of society as a whole.

George Weigel confirms this view in his biography of John Paul II. He describes the Pope's *Theology of the Body* as a *"theological time bomb* set to go off with dramatic consequences, sometime in the third millennium of the Church. When that happens," he continues, "perhaps in the twenty-first century, the theology of the body may well be seen as a critical moment not only in Catholic theology, but in the history of modern thought."[5]

I myself am frustrated by the fact that I didn't learn about the richness and sensibleness of the Church's teaching when I was growing up, despite twelve years of Catholic education. For the most part, the message was simply, "Don't do it." So what did I do? The exact opposite, of course.

Had I been taught how wonderful and beautiful the Catholic vision of sex and marriage actually is, perhaps I would have thought it something worth holding out for. Perhaps I would have been spared the pain I afflicted on myself and others. But when I speak of a merciful God who can forgive, heal, and restore us, it's not theory. I've lived it, and I continue, by God's grace, to grow closer to the light every day.

4. How can I regain this understanding of sex if I've already blown it?

In light of the redemption that Christ has won for us, nothing is completely "blown." Nothing we've ever done could possibly be more powerful than the cross of Christ. When Christ died, he took all our fallen humanity with him, and he rose from the dead so that we too could live a new life (see Rom 6:4).

Jesus became sin so that we might become the righteousness of God (see 2 Cor 5:21). This means there's always the possibility of "renewing our minds" (see Rom 12:2). There's always the possibility of conversion. There's always the possibility, no matter how deep in the pit we may be, of turning around, walking toward the light, and experiencing new life.

If I may paraphrase St. Paul's words to the Romans: I appeal to you, in view of God's mercy, to offer your sexuality as a living sacrifice, whole and entire to God. You need not conform any longer to the pattern of this world, but you can be transformed by the renewing of your mind. Then you will understand and desire God's will for your sexuality—his good, pleasing, and perfect will (see Rom 12:1-2). And living according to God's plan will bring you the joy and happiness for which you've been searching your whole life.

Everything else is a sham. Yes, Christ's teachings are difficult. We should never underestimate that difficulty. How many among us, by our own strength, are able to love our enemies? I have a hard enough time trying to love my friends. How many among us, by our own strength, are able *never* to lust in our hearts?

It seems there's a fundamental dilemma here. Christ holds out his will only for us to realize that we can't live up to it. And how does Christ respond? "With men this is impossible, but with God all things are possible" (Mt 19:26). Let's pray:

Lord, please help me. Give me the grace to trust you with my whole self—all that I am, body and soul. I give you my hopes and fears, my achievements and failings, my strengths and weaknesses, my sins, my longings, my desires—especially, right now, my sexual sins, longings, and desires. I lay them all at your feet. Help me to be the man (woman) you've created me to be. Renew my mind that I might see the great gift of sex and marriage as you've created them to be. I know I cannot live your will on my own, but I trust you to make up what I am lacking. Amen.

5. We're engaged. We know in our hearts we're already committed to each other for life. Why shouldn't we express that commitment through sexual intercourse?

Let's consider again what intercourse expresses. It's the visible (physical) expression of the invisible (spiritual) marriage bond. It's where the words of the wedding vows become flesh. It's the sign of the sacrament of marriage that, for Catholics, only comes about when bride and groom have exchanged valid consent in the presence of a priest or deacon and two witnesses. It's not merely an expression of a feeling in your hearts that you're "already committed."

That feeling is understandable. I remember how committed I felt to Wendy when we were engaged. It's true to say that at some level engaged couples are "already committed."

Committed to what? To getting married. Otherwise, they wouldn't be planning a wedding. Yet engaged couples must also recognize *they're not yet married*. Otherwise, they wouldn't be planning a wedding.

Despite how committed I felt to Wendy when we were engaged, she wasn't my wife until the Holy Spirit established the marriage bond between us. That didn't happen when I proposed to her and she said yes. It didn't happen when we met with our priest to discuss wedding dates and marriage preparation. It didn't happen when we booked the reception site and sent out our invitations. It didn't happen at the rehearsal in the Church the night before.

All these were clear indications that we were committed to getting married. But it wasn't an absolute or irrevocable commitment. We were both free to back out at any time up until the moment we exchanged consent at the altar. At that moment, the Holy Spirit established the marriage bond between us. When we consummated our marriage, we knew that we were sealing and completing the spiritual bond established between us earlier that day.

That's the joy of sacramental sex. Hold out for the real thing. If you've already had sex, there's no reason you can't stop now: go to confession (if you're Catholic), and wait until your physical union is an honest expression of the spiritual bond of marriage. This is one of the *best* things you can do to prepare for this wonderful sacrament.

6. My soon-to-be fiancé and I both have parents who divorced, so we decided to move in together to see if we're compatible before making any serious commitment. In our situation, that seemed like the smart thing to do. Why does the Church teach that we're "living in sin"?

At first glance, there seems a certain logic to the idea of "trying it out" before making the serious, permanent commitment of marriage. Nevertheless, as a growing body of social research has firmly established, "living together," rather than being a preparation for marriage, is more often preparation for divorce. Studies indicate a 50 percent higher risk of divorce for those who live together before marriage as compared with those who do not.[6]

This phenomenon can only be fully understood within the broader context of the widespread abandonment of Christian teaching on the meaning of sex. A cohabiting couple is "living in sin" not so much because they live under the same roof, but because it most often means they have made a public commitment to engage in sex outside of marriage. While sharing a common life in the same residence before marriage raises additional issues, the core problem is a misunderstanding and misuse of sex. Thus those who are sexually active before marriage without cohabiting are also at a much greater risk of divorce. One study, for example, concludes that marriages that began with premarital sex are three times more likely to end in divorce than those in which sex was saved until after the wedding.[7]

For most of us, society has robbed us of the tools to understand and embrace the true meaning of sex. We grow up in a world that has almost completely severed the inherent, God-given connection between sexual union and marriage. To many, the idea that a couple would marry as virgins seems archaic. In fact, it's not uncommon for both husband and wife to have already had multiple sexual partners before meeting each other.

None of this is outside the reach of Christ's redeeming, healing love. Yet, if this issue is left unaddressed, a couple who enters marriage having already engaged in sex with each other or with other people will *inevitably* face difficulties, perhaps totally unaware that the pain they're experiencing stems from the wounds of illicit sex. It's no coincidence that the dramatic rise in the divorce rate has coincided with the dramatic rise in sexual activity outside of marriage. I offer the following as some plausible reasons for the connection:

• Indulging in a sexual relationship which is dissoluble, uncommitted to lifelong fidelity, and closed to life[8] cannot prepare a couple to embrace a sexual relationship (marriage) that demands indissolubility, lifelong fidelity, and openness to life. By consistently choosing such behavior, the couple is demonstrating that they are, in fact, *ill-prepared* for the commitment of marriage because they've been psychologically "trained" in its opposite.

• Authentic love is ready to sacrifice everything for the good of the beloved. Above all, it never entices another to do evil. To engage in gravely disordered kinds of behavior and encourage one's beloved to do so as well manifests an attitude diametrically opposed to authentic love. At the very least, it manifests a blatant ignorance of the meaning and demands of that love, which must be the foundation of the sacrament of marriage.

• Willingness to engage in premarital sex demonstrates an implicit acceptance of sex outside the confines of marriage. Thus it should be no surprise that studies indicate much higher rates of adultery among couples who engaged in premarital sex as compared with those who don't.[9] Adultery is, of course, one of the main causes of divorce.

• Premarital sexual activity establishes a pattern of self-indulgence that fosters the very vices (lust, pride, selfishness, dishonesty, distrust, sloth, and more) that serve to undermine—and if not addressed, destroy—the healthy relationship of a husband and wife.

• The love required for the sacrament of marriage demands a profound purity, humility, selflessness, honesty, trust, and willingness to sacrifice that can be established *only* by embracing the virtue of chastity—that is, lived respect for the truth and meaning of sexuality outside *and within* marriage.

• Sexual intimacy clouds a couple's judgment of their relationship, preventing them from reaching the objective assessment essential to discerning an authentic vocation to marriage.

• By their choices, cohabiting couples and those that are otherwise sexually active deprive themselves of the fullness of God's grace in their lives. Without this grace it's impossible for a man and woman to love one another as they're called to—in imitation of Christ.

All these factors contribute to the disintegration of men and women as individuals and of any relationship they share. If left unaddressed, the attempt to establish a marriage on such patterns of relating is akin to building a house on sand (see Mt 7:26). But this shouldn't be cause for despair.

It doesn't matter how long a list of sins we have in our lives. Christ came not to condemn us but to save us. Christ can forgive us. Christ can restore us. Christ can heal our wounds. Christ can teach us how to love. But only if we let him.

So if you're truly serious about staying out of the divorce courts, turn to Christ and seek the grace that he will freely give you to live according to the truth of sex and marriage *now*. There's no better guarantee of a successful marriage than to train yourself in the virtues that are necessary for a successful marriage ahead of time. It's never too late to start. Go for it!

7. My boyfriend and I are very much in love and very attracted to each other. We haven't gone "all the way," but we find it hard to know where the line is. Is there a line?

Perhaps you remember your parish priest, CCD teacher, or mom drawing a line along the scale of physical behaviors and saying, "If you cross this, you've sinned." I'm not trying to discount the need for such physical "lines," but they often fail to do justice to the complexity of human hearts.

It's here that we experience the battle between love and lust. It's here that we decide which force within us will hold sway in our actions. So before the line is drawn along the scale of physical behaviors, it must be drawn in the human heart. This line applies to *everyone* in *every* situation and in *every* romantic relationship—married, engaged, or dating.

In his book *Love and Responsibility*, John Paul II speaks of the moral principle that should guide all human behavior. He calls it the *personalistic norm*. Stated negatively, it says that persons have such great dignity that never, under any circumstance, is it acceptable to *use* a person as a means to an end. Stated positively, the *personalistic norm* says that the only proper response to another person is that of *love*.

In John Paul II's mind, then, the opposite of love is not hatred. It's *use*. Here lies the battle for purity in physical manifestations of affection. We must resist every impulse in us that tends to treat other people as means to our own selfish gratification, so that we can learn to love others for their own sake.[10]

Again, this points to the need for a deep conversion of heart. Without the perspective of God's plan in the beginning and our redemption in Christ, almost all we know are the distortions that sin has caused in us. We consider it completely "normal" to use others for our own physical or emotional pleasure, so much so that we call it "love." Our society fosters this attitude, shamelessly encouraging it at every turn.

This is the very essence of the distortions that occur in man and woman's relationship.[11] If we are ever to discover and experience true love, we must win the battle in our hearts over lust, over any desire to use people for our own gratification. And this victory, of course, can only be accomplished through the help of God's grace.

Physical manifestations of affection, no matter where they fall on the scale—from holding hands and kissing to sexual intercourse—are meant to be outward signs that express genuine inward realities. When outward signs do express genuine inward realities, there's a corresponding physical and emotional satisfaction, from the tender comfort of holding hands to the explosive intensity of orgasm in intercourse.

These joys are God-given. They're some of the joys promised by Christ when he calls us to love as he loves, so that his joy might be in us and our joy might be complete (see Jn 15:11). Thus, those who love as Christ loves, and express that love in a manifestation of affection appropriate to the state of their relationship, should receive the joy that flows from that expression as a gift from God.

We cross the line in the heart, however, when we seek that physical and emotional satisfaction as an end in itself—when we treat another person, not as a person created for his or her own sake, but as a means to our own selfish ends. This can happen all too easily, even if we don't cross the line on the scale of physical behaviors.

For example, a married couple isn't "crossing the line" when they have intercourse. It's appropriate to their relationship. But if a married couple is having intercourse *merely* because "it feels good" and not because each wants to say what intercourse means ("I am yours freely, totally, faithfully, and, yes, I am open to children"), they've crossed the line in the heart. Similarly, a dating couple is not crossing the line of physical behaviors by holding hands or even kissing. But if a dating couple is holding hands or kissing *merely* because "it feels good" and not because they want to say what these expressions mean, they've crossed the line in the heart.

Admittedly, the meaning of holding hands or a kiss is not as universal or God-given as sexual intercourse. At a minimum, however, these behaviors mean (or should mean), "I respect you deeply as a person, I have tender affection for you, and I want to speak to you of your goodness." They should never be the expression of a desire to "get something" from the other for one's own ends. They should instead be expressions of a disinterested desire to affirm the other person for his or her own sake.

Discerning the inner movements of our hearts can be confusing and difficult. Because of our own fallenness, we'll inevitably recognize elements of self-seeking mixed in with otherwise genuine desires of love. This acknowledgment doesn't stifle expressions of affection. Instead, it leads to their ever purer realization.

Such genuineness in expressions of affection—from holding hands to sexual intercourse in marriage—is only possible as we surrender our whole selves as sexual beings, as men and women, to the transforming love of Christ. Without such surrender, we'll inevitably be stuck to one degree or another in a habit of using others, and for lack of knowledge of anything else, we'll make the tragic mistake of calling that "love."

8. I think I understand, but aren't there still physical lines that shouldn't be crossed?

Yes. But any attempt to draw them should not be an excuse to avoid the battle in our own hearts. Such avoidance is all too easy if we're relying solely on external lines. If we fight the interior battle honestly and courageously, our hearts will *know* the line not to cross and will not want to cross it, for our own good and the good of our beloved. That being said, I offer the following "lines" on the physical scale only as a way to help you honestly assess your own heart.

One obvious example of a line not to cross for an unmarried couple is sexual intercourse. If a couple were to claim that they had made an honest and courageous assessment of their hearts and then had come to the conclusion that they could engage in intercourse as a genuine expression of their relationship, they'd be fooling themselves. It's true that they could experience some elements of love in intercourse. There always remains an echo of truth even in our distorted expressions of love. But it's not true that the act itself would be an act of love. In fact, it could not avoid being an act of use instead.

Similarly, physical behaviors that aim to arouse the body in preparation for intercourse (fondling each other's genitals or breasts, and even some kinds of extended kissing and embracing) are not appropriate expressions of affection for the unmarried. When there is simply no moral possibility of consummated love, it is, in fact, *unloving* to arouse someone to the point of physical craving for intercourse. If we must talk about physical lines in order to keep our hearts honest, we can say this: if either the man or woman is brought to the verge of climax, or has reached climax, or is aroused to the point of being tempted to masturbate, such a couple "crossed the line" *a long time before* and is in serious need of examining their hearts and their motives.

As the expression goes, it's foolish (read: wrong, unloving, entirely inappropriate) to start the engine if you can't drive the car. A person brought to climax or tempted to masturbate has not only started the engine but has spent a long time revving it as well.

We're speaking here not just about a need to modify our behavior to fit some arbitrary moral code. We're speaking about the need of a deep transformation of our hearts from "loving" as the world "loves" to loving as Christ loves. Underneath all our distorted sexual expressions, there is something genuine that men and women are seeking. They're seeking love, physical closeness, intimacy, joy, and pleasure—in a word, happiness.

But how many (myself included) can attest to the emptiness, guilt, isolation, and despair that follow an illicit sexual experience? How many fail to find what they're truly looking for? We'll search in vain for happiness until we realize that what we're looking for can only be found in the One who created us.

God gave us sexual passion and desire—believe it or not—to point us to him. Lust and its satisfaction are a pale counterfeit for the true passion of love and the peace that floods the soul upon its discovery. If, through an ongoing conversion of heart, we surrender our lusts to Christ and allow him to transform them, we'll experience sexual desire as the desire to love as he loves. As all our expressions of affection become more and more Christlike, we actually discover what we failed to find previously.

Then, the simplest manifestation of affection—whether a look, a touch, or a gentle kiss—is more joyous and fulfilling than the most intense illicit sexual "encounter." Why? Because it's genuine. It's real. It's honest. It's true to what's appropriate in the given stage of the relationship.

It's not seeking to *get* anything. It's seeking to give and *affirm*. It's not interested in its own satisfaction. It's interested merely in loving the person for his or her own sake, and receiving the same love in return.

Such freedom and genuineness come at a high price—the price of the cross of Christ. Lust, pride, self-seeking, all must die in us if we're to rise to love: true love, pure love, the love for which we're all incessantly searching. The alternative to taking up our cross and following Christ (see Mt 10:38) is the desperate attempt to camouflage the void and disappointment in our souls by the fleeting pleasure of mutually exploitative orgasms. Only the most hardened heart can continue to feign solace in the afterglow of such an experience.

9. Isn't there some kind of difference between dating and engaged couples with regard to chastity?

As the *Catechism* states: "Those who are *engaged to marry* are called to live chastity in continence.... They should reserve for marriage the expressions of affection that belong to married love."[12] Still, it's right to recognize a degree of intimacy appropriate for engaged couples that isn't appropriate for those who are merely "dating."

Remember that physical manifestations of affection are meant to be outward signs that express inward realities. There's an inward reality present in the hearts of the engaged that isn't present in the hearts of those who are dating. As Fr. Paul Quay suggests in his insightful book, *The Christian Meaning of Human Sexuality*: "Those who are engaged, since they are committed to each other, even though not yet fully, have sufficient reason to manifest their love, even by prolonged kissing and embracing ... provided, of course, that this leads neither of them into sin [using the other for selfish gratification, for example], provided they do not get themselves violently overwrought [to the point of climax or temptation to masturbate, for example], and provided the engagement does not go on forever."[13]

His counsel is clearly not given as a license to "push the envelope." It assumes a mature Christian commitment and an experience of the freedom to which we're called in Christ Jesus (see Gal 5:1). This is the freedom to love, to see what is good, true, and beautiful, and to desire it with all one's heart.

Such freedom *always* chooses the good of others, rejecting utterly any temptation to violate that good. An engaged couple who knows this mature level of freedom is able to express their affection for one another without the least bit of fear that one would ever *use* the other for his or her own gratification, without the least bit of fear that one would ever push the envelope in order to see how much more he or she can "get."

To any doubter, let me say that this type of freedom is truly possible. I speak from experience. It calls, of course, for open and honest communication. It calls for care, as St. Paul cautioned, never to use our freedom to indulge the cravings of our fallen nature (see Gal 5:13). And while it's certainly true that we should never underestimate our weaknesses (conversion is ongoing), we should also never underestimate the power of the cross to set us free.

Unfortunately, we've been trained to think of ourselves as animals without control. So in order to stay chaste, some couples think it necessary never to be alone for any extended time before they get married. The fear is that if they *were* alone they wouldn't be able to say no to sex. This isn't freedom. Let's not take up again a yoke of slavery (see Gal 5:1).

Certainly, if a couple knows they'd do something wrong if they were alone, then they shouldn't be alone. (In traditional Catholic language, it's called "avoiding the near occasion of sin.") Those who make the sacrifices necessary to avoid temptations are to be commended. But if the only thing that kept a couple from having sex before they got married was the fact that they didn't have the opportunity, what does that say about the desire of their hearts? Do they *truly* desire the good? Are they truly *free*?

Freedom is essential to authentic marital love. If an engaged couple isn't capable of expressing their affection in ways that are genuine, true, and *free* (in a word, chaste), things won't automatically change when they get married. Without this freedom—which can only be achieved by experiencing the ever-deepening redemption of our sexuality in Christ—sexual activity will remain, at some level, exploitative, even if the couple doing it is married. Let's pray:

Lord Jesus, come into my deepest self. Transform my sexual desires into those of love. Make me chaste. Grant me a living experience of the freedom for which you died to set me free. Amen.

10. Does the Church really teach that masturbation is wrong? What about adolescents who are just experimenting?

Yes. Masturbation is always an objective disorder (see the next question for a further discussion of *why* it's wrong). Nevertheless, subjective responsibility for masturbation can be lessened by immaturity, the force of habit, conditions of anxiety, or other psychological factors.[14]

It's perfectly natural for adolescents to be curious about their maturing bodies. And the novelty of hormone surges can be a powerful temptation to experiment with masturbation. This is understandable. But it doesn't change the objective fact that masturbation is a disorder. It's not in keeping with our great dignity as men and women who are called to love as God loves.

While those stuck in a habit of masturbation must be shown compassion, it's a service to no one to water down the truth. By doing so we only keep people in their chains. Christ has redeemed us. This means it's truly possible to live according to the full truth of our sexuality.

11. Most psychologists speak of masturbation as a normal, healthy thing. They even indicate that it's unhealthy *not* to masturbate. Why doesn't the Church just get with it?

We must realize that without the perspective of God's plan in the beginning, and without understanding that Christ came into the world to restore that plan, we'll inevitably be looking at our experience of sexual desire through the lens of our fallen humanity. From *this* perspective, masturbation does seem like a "normal" and even "healthy" thing.

It's "normal" to be sexually aroused, right? It's "normal" to want to "relieve" sexual tension, right? If you have an itch, you don't just let it drive you crazy—you scratch it, right? In fact, only the oddball would choose to endure the itch without scratching it, right? So it could actually be "unhealthy" to let sexual tension build up without "relieving" it, right?

There's a certain logic here. In fact, it's virtually impossible to understand why masturbation is wrong within this paradigm. What's needed—not just to understand the masturbation issue but in order to understand the truth of sexuality and, in turn, the true meaning of love and life—is a complete paradigm shift.

We've inherited a worldview (modern rationalism) that's closed in on itself. We're all a bunch of *omphaloskeptics* (a fancy word for "navel-gazers"). We can't see beyond the physical and visible to the spiritual and invisible. We can't see beyond the temporal and immanent to the eternal and transcendent.

We look at the stars, and rather than pondering the expansive grandeur of the Creator, we reduce the universe to mathematical equations. We encounter another body, and rather than seeing the revelation of a person made in the image and likeness of God, we see a *thing* to use and consume for our own gratification. We encounter the deep waters of sexual desire, and rather than seeing our call to share in the divine mystery by swimming in the pure waters of life-giving love with an "other," we dive headfirst into our own shallow, stagnant swamp and get stuck in the sludge of self-indulgent isolation.

As we've noted, sex is symbolic. It's meant to be an efficacious sign of God's free, total, faithful, fruitful love. It's meant to be a human participation in the divine Communion of Persons. Yes, sex is meant to point us beyond the stars to Ultimate Reality—God.

Masturbation, however easy a habit it is to fall into, only throws us back on ourselves. It exemplifies a worldview devoid of the transcendent *otherness* of God. It symbolizes self-pity, fear of abandoning oneself to another, and the utter sterility of isolation.

It's the antithetical expression of our call to image God in a life-giving communion of persons. Masturbation epitomizes the inversion of sexual desire caused by original sin. What is it but self-seeking, self-gratifying sexual indulgence?

Such behavior speaks very pointedly about a person's concept of his or her own sexuality and, in turn, about his or her whole person. It speaks of an anxiety toward self and others, an inner frustration with the truth of one's own being, and an unwillingness or inability to make a sincere gift of self to another. The fantasy life that often accompanies masturbation speaks of a dissatisfaction with and withdrawal from reality.

If one who struggles with masturbation is ever to enter marriage lovingly and fruitfully, it's utterly essential that he or she overcome this habit through perseverance, prayer, the sacraments, God's grace, and perhaps the guidance of a wise spiritual director. Why? If one's sexual impulse is conditioned by self-indulgence rather than self-giving, and if the pleasure of orgasm is divorced in one's mind from the risk of loving an "other" and the responsibility of fertility, then standing at an altar and pronouncing vows will do little if anything to undo that condition.

A man who's been trained by a habit of masturbation, for example, will simply transfer his self-indulgent impulse onto his wife. He'll have sex with a fantasy rather than with the real woman he married. Is that love? Can that ever be an expression of the marriage bond and a renewal of wedding vows?

Psychologists who promote masturbation, and those who accept their advice, have been duped. Let's cry out to God for the grace to pierce through our fears, our anxieties, our inner frustrations. Let's endure the pain of allowing God to reverse our inversions.

Only then will we know the true joy and satisfaction we're looking for. It's not self-satisfaction. It's the satisfaction of sacrificing all in the risk of love. It's the satisfaction of holding out for the real thing—the encounter with an "other" that's meant to prepare us for the ultimate encounter with the Ultimate Other: God.

12. What am I supposed to do with all my sexual feelings and desires if I can't have sex and I'm not supposed to masturbate? Sometimes I feel as if I'm going to explode.

This is a good place to address the difference between the repression of sexual desire and its redemption. Most people who are trying to live a chaste life fall into the mistake of "stuffing" their sexual feelings or trying to ignore them by sweeping them under the rug. The problem is, they keep coming back, and usually with more force than they had in the first place.

Sexual feelings and desires are extremely powerful. Repressing them is *not* the answer. In order to know true freedom and put our sexuality at the service of authentic love, we must experience the redemption of our sexuality. Our sexual desires need to be transformed in Christ so that we can experience them as God intended in the beginning (see chapter one).

Because of the rupture between body and soul caused by original sin, we've all inherited disordered sexual desires.[15] They can be difficult, if not seemingly impossible at times, to control. So we need to ask ourselves: Am I in control of my sexual desires, or are they in control of me? If they're in control of us, then we're not free.

We also need to ask ourselves: What's the sentiment or character of these desires? Are they at the service of authentic love, or are they simply a desire for selfish gratification?

When sexual feelings, desires, and temptations present themselves, as they inevitably do, instead of trying to ignore them or "stuff" them by pushing them down and under, we need to bring them up and out. Not up and out in the sense of indulging them, but up and out and into the hands of Christ our Redeemer. You might simply say a prayer such as this:

Lord Jesus, I give to you my sexual desires. Please undo in me what sin has done so that I might know freedom in this area and experience sexual desire as you intend. Amen.

The more we invite Christ into our passions and desires and allow him to purify them, the more we find we're able to exercise proper control of them. And we begin more and more to experience our sexuality, not as the desire for selfish gratification but as the desire to give ourselves away in imitation of Christ. This is what redemption is all about.

But it's not easy. To be sure, it can be an intense spiritual battle (see Eph 6:12). Allowing Christ to purify us involves a real death to our passions. It involves being crucified with Christ so that we might be raised with him to a new life (see Rom 6)—a new life in which we find ourselves more and more able to love as he loves, which is what our sexuality is all about.

In fact, as powerfully as the fallen sex drive leads us toward selfish gratification at the expense of others, even more powerfully does God want the redeemed sex drive to lead us toward the freedom of loving others as Christ loves us. Sexual desire is meant to lead us to the fulfillment of the gospel. This is why Pope John Paul II describes the sexual urge as "a vector of aspiration along which [our] whole existence develops and perfects itself from within."[16]

True love and true freedom are possible. But we don't arrive at them overnight. It can be a long and difficult road. Nevertheless, paraphrasing John Paul II, Christ calls us to learn with perseverance and consistency the true meaning of sex. He calls us to understand the inner movements of our hearts so that we can distinguish between what, on the one hand, constitutes sexual attraction as God intended it and what, on the other hand, bears only the sign of lust.

And although these different movements of the heart can, within certain limits, be confused with one another, Christ calls us to discern the difference. Again, this is difficult, but as John Paul II adds, "This task *can* be carried out, and is really worthy of Man."[17]

So what do you do with all your sexual desires and feelings? Give them to Christ and allow him to work this miracle of redemption in you. The only thing that will explode is your concept of sex. In God's plan it's more awesome than we as fallen human beings could possibly imagine.

Another important thing to remember: This redemption isn't just for those who don't have a "legitimate outlet" for their sexual desires. It's for everyone, married people included. Marriage in no way legitimizes spouses' using one another just to "relieve" their disordered sexual desires. They too must experience the redemption of their sexuality if their lovemaking is to be just that— making *love* and not making *lust*.

Here are some additional prayers you may find helpful as you seek to grow day by day in the true freedom of the redemption of your sexuality.

A Prayer for Purity of Heart

Lord, you have created me in your image and likeness as a man [woman]. Help me to accept and receive my sexuality as a gift from you. You have inscribed in my very being, in my sexuality, the call to love as you love, in sincere self-giving, and you have made the "one flesh" union of man and woman in marriage a sign of your own life and love in the world. Grant me the grace always to resist the many lies that con-

*tinually assail the truth and meaning of this great gift of sexuality.
Grant me purity of heart so that I might see the image of your glory in
the beauty of others, and one day see you face to face. Amen.*

A Prayer in a Moment of Temptation to Lust

*This is a woman [man] made in the image and likeness of God, never
to be looked upon as an object for my gratification. Lord Jesus, grant me
the grace to see the image of your glory in the beauty of this woman
[man], and order my sexual desires toward the truth of love. I renounce
any tendency within me to use others for my own pleasure, and I unite
my sufferings with yours on the cross. Amen.*

13. Should I feel guilty if I have wet dreams?

No, because there is no moral fault involved here. Ejaculating involuntarily
in your sleep is of a different nature altogether from intentionally stimulating
yourself to orgasm.

14. What's the big deal with pornography?

Pornography is attractive. That reality should not be denied or dismissed.
Instead, we need to ask why. Why *is* it so darned alluring? How is it that it can
reach in and get such a grip on our souls that it seems to suck us in with irre-
sistible force?

I'm speaking from a man's perspective, of course. Visual pornography is predominantly a male thing. It taps into the way men are wired much more than
into the way women are. This is why *Playgirl* magazine is purchased much
more by men with same-sex attraction than by women. Most women simply
don't get their "kicks" by looking at pictures of naked men.[18]

What's the big deal with pornography? Again, if we're stuck only in our
fallen perspective and our fallen desires—nothing. It's completely "normal."
It's "natural." But if we recognize even the faintest echo in our hearts of God's
original plan for sexuality, we see that pornography epitomizes how far we
have fallen from it.

If we're ever to discover true love, true joy, true happiness, we must redis-
cover the "nuptial meaning of the body" and live according to it (see chapter
one). We must die to our lusts and experience the redemption of our bodies, of
our sexuality in Christ. This is the only path to true human fulfillment.

Experiencing this redemption is not a minor point of the gospel message,
it's not merely an appendix of the gospel message, it *is* the gospel message. As

John Paul II says, rediscovery of the nuptial meaning of the body always means rediscovery of the meaning of the whole of existence, the meaning of life.[19] "This is, in fact, the perspective of the whole Gospel, of the whole teaching, in fact, of the whole mission of Christ."[20]

What's the big deal with pornography? It robs us of the very meaning of life. It's an anti-gospel message, because it seeks to foster precisely those distortions of our sexual desires that we must struggle *against* in order to discover true love.

What's the big deal with pornography? If lust is a fire that we must allow Christ to extinguish, pornography is the fan for the flame. No amount of rationalization, no number of excuses that "it's normal" or that "men will be men," can change what pornography is and what it does to the way men think of women (and women think of themselves).[21] If men are to be men, they must learn how to love women. They must learn how to see them not as *things* for their sexual gratification but as *persons* made in the image of God.

What's the big deal with pornography? It does nothing but foster in a man his fallen inclination to treat women as things for his own sexual gratification. A man who uses pornography, so long as he remains in its clutches, has incapacitated himself to love women properly.

So long as he remains in its clutches, he cannot hope to have a healthy, pure relationship with a woman. He cannot hope to enter marriage honestly, fruitfully, and faithfully. Men who use pornography have emasculated themselves.

This is not because the naked body is bad. Nor, for that matter, is it bad to desire to see images of the naked body. What's wrong is the lust in the human heart and the desire to foster that lust. What's wrong is portraying the naked body in a way that intentionally incites lust and reduces a human being to an object to gratify that lust.

As an antidote to this lust, we might do well to ponder the naked figures painted by Michelangelo in the Sistine Chapel. In fact, as part of the restoration project of the Sistine Chapel, Pope John Paul II called for the removal of several loin cloths that prudish clerics had had painted over these figures. Why? John Paul believes that an artist who understands the nuptial meaning of the body can portray the naked body in a way that helps us see the true beauty of our being created as male and female in the image of God.

Such an appreciation of our dignity, while clearly the intent of Michelangelo, is clearly *not* the intent of Hugh Hefner and Larry Flint. So from John Paul's perspective, the problem with pornography is not that it reveals too much of a person but that it reveals too little.

There's a deep, insatiable longing in the human soul to know and understand the meaning of masculinity and femininity. Tragically, very few people grow up with appropriate and chaste ways of expressing and meeting this God-given need. Void of the truth, it's all too easy to succumb to the lies, to seek to meet legitimate needs and curiosities in terribly distorted ways.

This is why pornography is so darned attractive. This is why there are more hard-core pornography stores in the United States than there are McDonald's restaurants. This is why the large majority of traffic on the Internet is pornographic. This is why pornography is a multi-*billion*-dollar-per-year industry in the United States alone.

The antidote to pornography is to fill that deep interior need for revelation of the meaning of sexuality with the truth. When we see the truth of sexuality, the profound mystery of God's plan revealed through our bodies, we find what we've been looking for our whole lives. When we find the truth, the lies no longer attract because we see them as the empty counterfeits they are.

Praise God! The true beauty of real men and real women is far more satisfying and glorious than the computer-altered glossy prints of pornography. We need to ask God to give us the eyes to see it. We must pray for the virtue of purity, which John Paul II describes as the glory of God revealed through the body.[22] "Blessed are the pure in heart, for they shall see God"—in the body (see Mt 5:8).

If you're stuck in a habit of pornography use, if you've been exposed to pornography at any time in your life and are seeking to undo its effects, if you're the wife, girlfriend, or fiancée of a man using pornography, don't despair. Go for help.[23] You'll find that there is hope, and you can be healed.

Five

"I Do"-ing It

Chastity Within Marriage

In the spiritual life of married couples there are at work the gifts of the Holy Spirit, especially the ... gift of respect for what is a work of God. This gift, together with love and chastity, ... leads to understanding, among the possible "manifestations of affection," the singular, or rather the exceptional, significance of [the conjugal] act.

Pope John Paul II[1]

If you're married—or are getting married soon, or would someday like to be married—you need to answer each of the following questions.

- Do you intend to be faithful to your wedding vows?
- No matter how difficult it may be to remain faithful, do you *still* intend to be faithful to your wedding vows?
- No matter how much you may have to challenge your own ways of thinking and acting to remain faithful, do you *still* intend to be faithful to your wedding vows?
- No matter how much sacrifice is necessary, no matter how much you may need to call upon God's grace to remain faithful, do you *still* intend to be faithful to your wedding vows?

I trust that you answered *yes* to all these questions. They aren't asking **any**thing more of you than what you've already committed to, or plan on committing to someday, at the altar—to live your vows honestly and truly in good times and bad, through thick and thin, no matter what the cost, until death. Two more questions:

- How healthy do you think a marriage would be in which the spouses were regularly unfaithful to their wedding vows, and thus continually demonstrated their lack of commitment to them?
- Conversely, how healthy do you think a marriage would be in which the spouses regularly renewed their vows to one another, and every time they did so, strengthened their commitment to them?

One of the main points of this book so far has been to demonstrate that sex is only sex to the extent that it participates in the "I do" of wedding vows. (You may want to review chapter three for a discussion of what you're saying "I do" to). Anything less is a cheap counterfeit for the love that we long for and deserve as men and women made in the image and likeness of God. This chapter is devoted to explaining what fidelity to the wedding vows means, practically speaking, in the sexual relationship of spouses. Then the following two chapters continue the discussion.

No doubt fidelity to the demands of love is challenging. But I would urge you: *let it challenge you.* Have the moral courage to be faithful to the demands of love no matter what the cost, no matter what the difficulty, no matter what the sacrifice. Have the courage to stand firm on the *yes* with which, I assume, you responded to the above questions. And have the courage to be consistent no matter where that consistency takes you.

See it through. Don't duck. Don't bow out. Don't look for excuses. Don't try to rationalize. Allow yourself to feel the agony of accepting the demands of love. As you pass through this agony, you'll come to discover the tranquility of *freedom.*

1. Why do married couples need the virtue of chastity when the wait is over?

It's a common but mistaken notion that the Church calls people to be chaste *until* marriage. But if we really understand what the virtue of chastity is, we'll recognize that such a statement implies that married people don't need to love each other. Chastity is not the same thing as abstinence. As we've noted earlier, chastity is the virtue that frees all our sexual thoughts, desires, and behaviors from self-seeking and orders them toward the truth of authentic love. So if spouses are truly to love one another, the virtue of chastity isn't an option—it's an absolute requirement.

Everyone is called to be chaste because everyone is called to love. The way chastity is expressed, of course, depends upon a person's state in life. For the unmarried person, it *does* mean abstinence from sex, because that's what authentic love calls for among the unmarried.

For the married person, however, it means that all sexual expression must be an honest expression of the marriage commitment. Any type of behavior that would contradict the free, total, faithful, and potentially fruitful self-giving to which the spouses commit at the altar would be an affront to the very meaning of sex. In other words, it would be a violation of chastity.

2. I've been married sixteen years and never thought about chastity *within* marriage, or about sex as a renewal of our wedding vows. What does chastity within marriage mean, practically speaking?

Regardless of how old you are or how long you've been married, it's never too late to grow in your understanding and your living out of the true meaning of sex. We have a patient, merciful God who wants to draw us ever closer in a nuptial relationship with himself. For married couples, growing in the true sacramental nature of their sexual relationship is one of the main ways they grow closer to God, as well as to each other.

The effort to make sex a true union of persons, a true sacrament of God's love (rather than just a means of selfish gratification), presents what John Paul II has called "the internal problem of every marriage."[2] It's much like the sacrament of love we find in the Eucharist. This act, too, is the consummation of a marriage, our marriage with Christ. If we receive Christ's Body worthily, it becomes the very source (in union with baptism) of divine life, holiness, and joy in our lives. If we don't receive Christ's Body worthily, we eat and drink our own condemnation because we're mocking what the Eucharist is (see 1 Cor 11:27-29). We're going through the motions, but we don't *mean* what we're saying.

Similarly, if husband and wife receive each other's bodies worthily in their sexual relationship, their sexual union becomes the very source of life, holiness, and joy in their marriage. But if spouses are just going through the motions and don't *mean* what they're saying—or worse yet, are in some way trying to *cancel* what the act means—then sexual union becomes the source of a fundamental disquiet in their marriage that, over time, will serve subtly (or not so subtly) to eat away at their relationship from the inside out. Again, it's no coincidence that the dramatic rise in the divorce rate in our country has coincided with the widespread abandonment of the Christian sexual ethic. So it's hard to underestimate how important the virtue of chastity is to a marriage.

How do you live it, practically speaking? To answer this question, we need to take a look at each of the elements of the marriage commitment. A valid marriage must be (1) free, (2) total, (3) faithful, and (4) open to children. These are the commitments that spouses must renew when they have sex. Let's look at each.

Free. Any way that a husband or wife might manipulate or coerce a spouse to have sexual relations would be a violation of the freedom of their union. A clear example would be "marital rape." Yet we're not talking only about such an extreme situation. The true freedom of love is also violated when spouses use sex as a tool in their relationship for some other end.

Perhaps sex is employed to gain power or control in the relationship. Perhaps it's offered as a "reward" for something else or withheld as a "punishment." None of this kind of behavior says, "I want to give myself to you freely to affirm your goodness and our marriage commitment."

Freedom is also violated, or you might say is nonexistent, when sex is engaged in merely as a response to a compulsive "need" for gratification. Freedom means there is a choice before you to which you can say yes or no. If you can't say no, your yes is emptied of its meaning. We're called to gain increasing self-mastery so that our passions don't control us, but we control them.

Total. The climax of the sexual act shouts loudly and clearly, "Take me. I'm totally yours. I'm holding nothing back." That ecstatic moment reflects the unreserved surrender of our persons and the unreserved receptivity of the other. To the degree that we knowingly and intentionally reserve any part of ourselves from our spouse in the sexual act, we cannot speak of a *total* self-giving.

Perhaps one spouse is emotionally distant from or cold toward the other. Perhaps both spouses are deliberately refusing to be transparent and vulnerable with each other. Perhaps they're not giving themselves to each other in climax at all. Such is the case when one or the other spouse intentionally seeks orgasm apart from the act of normal intercourse.

The acts by which spouses lovingly prepare each other for genital intercourse (foreplay) are honorable and good. But stimulation of each other's genitals to the point of climax apart from an act of normal intercourse is nothing other than mutual masturbation. There's no gift of self, no marital communion taking place at all. Nor are such acts open to conception.

An important point of clarification is needed. Since it's the male orgasm that's inherently linked with the possibility of new life, the husband must never *intentionally* ejaculate outside of his wife's vagina (unintended ejaculation involves no moral fault). Since the female orgasm, however, isn't necessarily linked to the possibility of conception, so long as it takes place within the overall context of an act of intercourse, it need not, morally speaking, be during actual penetration.

Ideally, the wife's orgasm would happen simultaneously with her husband's, but this is easier said than done for many couples. In fact, if the wife's orgasm isn't achieved during the natural course of foreplay and consummation, it would be the loving thing for the husband to stimulate his wife to climax thereafter (if she so desired).

Faithful. Spouses must be faithful to each other not only in action but also in thought. For example, fantasizing about someone else while engaging in sexual relations with your spouse would be a blatant violation of fidelity. Right at the moment when spouses should be expressing their unyielding fidelity to each other, they would actually be committing "adultery in their heart" (see Mt 5:28) with someone else.

This is one of the reasons that the use of pornography is so devastating to a marriage. It does nothing but feed and foster this type of infidelity.

Open to children. In the 1968 encyclical *Humanae Vitae*, Pope Paul VI reaffirmed the constant teaching of the Catholic Church that "each and every marriage act must remain open to the transmission of life." Perhaps a better way to understand this statement is that spouses must never do anything of their *own will* to close any act of intercourse to the transmission of life.

Yes, this means that use of any and all methods of contraception is a direct violation of a couple's wedding vows. This is perhaps the most contested and misunderstood teaching of the Catholic Church. For that reason, the entirety of chapter six will be devoted to clarifying it.

3. Are you saying that the only time you have sex with your wife is when you want to have a baby?

No. I'm saying that the only time I have sex with my wife is when we want to renew our marriage commitment. It's a myth that the Church teaches sex is *only* for babies, or that the only justifiable reason to have sex is when you want a baby. Some thinkers within the Church (such as St. Augustine) did mistakenly give this impression.

Furthermore, the long-standing formulation that procreation is the "primary end" of sexual union has often been misunderstood to mean procreation is the *only* end, or the only *good* end, of sexual union. But this has never been the official teaching of the Church. In fact, John Paul II says that if the *only* reason you're having sex with your spouse is because you want a baby, then you may be in danger of using your spouse as a means to an end, rather than loving your spouse as a person.[3]

I remember very clearly that the priest asked me and my bride at the altar if we would receive children lovingly from God, to which we individually responded, "I will." So fidelity to our vows demands that we never *intentionally impede* the possibility of pregnancy when we choose to express those vows through intercourse. In other words, while it's not necessary (and, in fact, could be unloving) to resolve that "we are having sex in order to have a baby," we must, in order to be faithful to our wedding vows, say: "In having sex, we know that we could have a baby, and we are willing to receive that baby lovingly from God." As John Paul II has concluded, "That approach alone is compatible with love and makes it possible to share the experience of love."[4] (Chapter six will provide a detailed discussion of this issue.)

4. Someone told me the Church teaches that oral sex is wrong even for married couples. Is that true?

It seems there are many troubled consciences out there looking for sound guidance on this issue. I'd even guess that the first thing many readers did when they got this book was to look up this question. (If you're one of them, be sure to read the rest of the book to understand better the context of this answer.)

So what does the Church teach? It depends on what you mean by "oral sex."

There's nothing that singles out the genitals as being "unkissable" as part of a husband and wife's foreplay to intercourse. The term "oral sex," however, most often refers to acts in which orgasm is sought and achieved *apart* from an act of intercourse. Indeed, many couples consider such behavior a desirable *alternative* to normal intercourse. And, yes, this is wrong, even for married couples—though the clarification made above regarding female orgasm is applicable here as well: It's not objectively wrong if the wife achieves climax as a result of oral stimulation, so long as it's within the context of a completed act of intercourse.

Oral copulation (that is, to the point of ejaculation) is simply *not* marital. It effects no *communion of persons* between the spouses. It's the consummation of nothing. It involves a severance of the pleasure of orgasm from the responsibility of fertility. It fosters a husband's tendency to objectify his wife. For these reasons, it does not and cannot symbolize and participate in the free, total, faithful, and fruitful love of God. It does not and cannot symbolize the marriage bond or renew a couple's vows.

Furthermore, while there's nothing wrong *per se* with oral stimulation of the genitals as foreplay to intercourse, such expressions require the greatest degree of purity and reverence so as never to degrade the goodness of marital intimacy. This kind of purity *is* possible, but it's also quite easy (especially for men, I'd say) to cross the line between love and lust, between intimately affirming the goodness of each other's bodies (and receiving that affirmation) and merely seeking to gratify base desire at each other's expense. As the saying goes, "from the sublime to the ridiculous is but a step." Spouses must always be sensitive to how easily they could take that step if they are to avoid it.[5]

It should go without mentioning that a spouse who is uncomfortable with such behavior should never be pressured into performing it. (Again, for whatever reason, it's usually husbands who exert pressure upon their wives.) Pressure exerted on a spouse to perform acts with which he or she is uncomfortable—even if they're not objectively wrong—indicates lack of respect for that spouse. It's a clear indication of having long since crossed the line between genuine love and self-seeking.

5. What about anal sex?

Again, it depends what you mean by the term. A husband should never intentionally ejaculate anywhere but in his wife's vagina. There's nothing *inherently* wrong with anal penetration as foreplay to normal intercourse. Still, there are some important health and aesthetic considerations that can't be overlooked.

Pardon the frankness, but vaginal penetration following anal penetration would be so unsanitary as to require some thorough anti-bacterial cleansing of the husband's penis to avoid health risks. There are other health considerations as well. The anus and rectum are simply not biologically designed to accommodate a penis. Penile penetration can cause trauma to the rectal wall (for example, tearing or bruising). Not a few people who engage in "anal sex" on a regular basis have bowel problems.

Furthermore, the excretory function of the rectum raises some basic aesthetic questions. What does anal penetration symbolize? Is this an act of beauty? Is it truly loving to subject one's wife to the health risks? Why would a couple want anal penetration to be part of their foreplay to normal intercourse on any kind of regular basis? What desire does it purport to satisfy?

Since anal penetration is in so many ways a parody of vaginal intercourse, I'd pose the following question to those who are attracted to it as a form of foreplay: Why not just skip that step with all its health risks and uncleanliness and enjoy the real thing with your spouse as God designed it?

6. This all sounds so mechanical, as if expressing love were just about plumbing and the insertion of body parts into the proper orifice.

If we have a split view of the body and soul—one that sees the spiritual element of our humanity as the "real person" and the body as just a "shell"—then, yes, what we've been discussing seems rather mechanical. Such a dualistic view of the human person logically concludes that "love" is expressed on a purely "spiritual level" and need not be bothered by the proper placement of certain body parts. The logic is sound, but it's based on a heretical view of the human person, a view that is absolutely irreconcilable with Christian anthropology (a Christian view of human nature).

As we noted in previous chapters, the body is the revelation of the person. We're not persons *in* a body. We're body-persons. The body *expresses* the soul. It makes visible the invisible.

What we do with our bodies we do with *ourselves*. What we do with our bodies reveals the sentiments of our heart. What we do with our bodies can determine whether we're expressing genuine love or merely some cheap imitation of it.

From this perspective, we're not just talking about mechanics—making sure you put body parts in the right place. We're talking about a husband and wife who, through the integrity of their bodies and souls, are loving each other as God loves—in a life-giving communion of persons. We're talking about husband and wife expressing their marriage commitment and becoming a sacramental sign of Christ's union with the Church.

What brings this sacramental communion about? Only that act by which the spouses become "one flesh." To be specific, only the inseminating union of genitals performed in a "human manner" in which the possibility of a new life is always left in the hands of the Creator.[6]

When we properly understand the indivisibility of body and soul—that the body expresses the person—we understand that this union of genitals is not merely a union of body parts. It's the means by which two body-persons image God by becoming *one* in a life-giving communion.

There's something in the average person that rises up against this teaching. There certainly was in me when I first heard it. *What's the big deal with seek-*

ing orgasm apart from intercourse, so long as it's with my own wife! I thought.

But then another question came to mind. Why would I *want* to seek orgasm apart from normal intercourse with my wife? Looking for honest answers in my own heart, I had to conclude that I wanted the pleasure of orgasm apart from any risk of becoming a father. There was simply no other substantial reason.

It's Christ who teaches us what love is. True love involves abandonment to the will of the Father. It involves willingness to accept a lifetime of responsibility.

True love involves risk. It involves sacrifice, pain—in a word, suffering. If we don't think so, we haven't spent much time looking at a crucifix. This is the heavenly Bridegroom giving up his body for his Bride. And husbands are called to love their wives "as Christ loved the Church" (Eph 5:25).

What's our typical reaction? "No! I don't want to. I want the pleasure without the responsibility, without the risk, without the suffering." I came to see very clearly that I resisted the Church's teaching because it cornered me into accepting the cross of Christ—as it should.

I once heard a bishop explain that marriage involves four rings: the engagement ring, two wedding rings, and "suffer-ring." As Fr. Paul Quay says, "It is just this link between true love and suffering that is rejected by sexual sin."[7] The honest person cannot fail to see the truth of this statement. If we reject the cross of Christ, if we refuse to take the risk of loving as Christ loves, we will still eventually end up with what we resisted—suffering. But the suffering that comes from resisting the cross is fruitless, empty, and despairing, while the suffering that comes from embracing the cross leads to the joy of the resurrection, the joy of love and new life.

O God, have mercy. Have mercy on me for the ways that I resist the pain of your cross. Help me to stop running from you. Help me to stop resisting the risk and the responsibility of love. Give me the grace to embrace your cross in my own life. Give me the grace to love my spouse as you love yours, the Church. I trust you to give me strength in my weakness. Amen.

7. Is the "missionary position" the only acceptable way for Catholics to have sex?

For readers who are unfamiliar with the term, the "missionary position" refers to intercourse in which the husband is on top of his wife, while she's on her back facing him. Stories vary, but it seems it was so named because missionaries promoted this as the "proper" position among native peoples they evangelized, discouraging other positions as impersonal and animal-like.

While no position for intercourse is wrong in and of itself, still (if the story is accurate) those missionaries had a point. It's telling, for example, that people speak of rear-entry intercourse as doing it "doggy-style." Such descrip- tions betray a less-than-personal approach to sex. It doesn't mean this position is inherently wrong, but uniting face-to-face instead can't help but promote the personal character of the spouses' union.

If you remember our discussion of the Book of Genesis, Adam discovered his difference from the animals specifically in his *sexuality*—his call to love through the body. But what was the first result of original sin? Adam and Eve hid from each other and from God.

Whatever it was they did, it was something below their dignity as human beings. In some sense, they stooped to the level of animals. Husband and wife should do everything possible in their sexual relationship to promote a truly personal and intimate union between them rather than stooping to the level of merely satisfying instinct as animals do.

I once heard it said that intimacy means "into-me-see." If husband and wife are intentionally hiding their faces from each other during sex, then some- thing's wrong. They should be able to look deeply into each other's eyes right at that most vulnerable moment—yes, right at the moment of climax—and rejoice in the mystery of *knowing* one another so intimately. Every person is an inexhaustible mystery. If sex is approached with the goal of coming to *know* the mystery of your spouse ever more fully as a person (as Adam *knew* his wife, Eve—see Gn 4:1), then position is superfluous.

8. What's wrong with trying to spice up your sex life with a little variety?

Candlelight, making a nice atmosphere, wearing an attractive nightgown, variety in location and position, can certainly add to the overall experience. Few would deny that. But truly "good" sex has nothing *essential* to do with these things.

The most fulfilling sex possible comes when husband and wife uncondi- tionally surrender themselves to each other—and receive each other—in a completely naked and honest revelation of their *persons*. If sex is not delving into the inexhaustible mystery of the other *person*, the "partners" in the exchange will inevitably grow bored. The way society trains us to think about sex breeds such boredom. Hence there are thousands of "sex manuals" on the market today intended to help couples spice up their sex life.

For the most part, these manuals offer suggestions that, if followed, would make what transpires in the marital bedroom resemble a scene from a porno flick rather than help a couple experience and participate in God's love. If a husband has to have his wife dress up like a porn star in order to be "turned on"; if a couple continually has to seek new and ever more contorted positions in order to avoid boredom; if spouses must become mere actors role-playing the script of one or the other's fantasy life in order to "perform"; if a couple is continually looking for new "techniques" to maximize physical pleasure instead of ever more loving ways to solidify marital union, then something is dreadfully amiss.[8]

If you really want "good sex," start by inviting God—who *is* love—to be with you. (Don't worry; God won't blush. He created sex.) Keep the lights on. Consciously renew your wedding vows with the language of your bodies. Mean what you say, and say what you mean.

Surrender your whole self *unconditionally* to your spouse. Receive your spouse *unconditionally*. As you do, look deeply and steadily into each other's eyes and thank God for the joy you know in being made in his image as you explode in the ecstasy of a true communion of persons.

9. Doing things the moral way sure does seem to take away the spontaneity. Why can't even married couples just go with the passion of the moment?

We've spoken a lot about the need for a total paradigm shift in order to understand the truth and meaning of sex—about the need to look to God's plan in the beginning, the disordering of our passions caused by original sin, and the redemption of our sexuality in Christ. If a husband and wife spontaneously follow their disordered passions, their love for each other will be overshadowed by self-seeking. They will inevitably end up using each other.

The Church's teaching does take away from *this* kind of spontaneity, as it should. But at the same time, Christ calls us to a different, much more fulfilling kind of spontaneity, a spontaneity that comes when we've made the concerted effort to train ourselves in the truth of love. Through the ongoing appropriation of our redemption in Christ, the very character of our sexual desires is transformed.

The more we've experienced this transformation, the more the desire to make a sincere gift of ourselves will well up within us—and with an intensity much more refined and noble than mere lust can ever rouse. Couples *should* follow the passion of such a moment—with joy and utter abandon. For in doing so, they'll abandon themselves spontaneously according to the demands of love.

I once heard it explained this way: An untrained person can "spontaneously" bang away on a piano keyboard with the satisfaction of having made some noise. But in the end, that's all it is—meaningless noise. On the other hand, when a concert pianist "spontaneously" tickles the keys, he produces sounds of beauty capable of lifting the soul to the heavens and beyond. But as we all know, behind the beauty of the music is a lifetime of self-discipline and training, a lifetime of concerted effort in perfecting his skill.

The effort needed to "make beautiful music" spontaneously through sexual union is no less demanding. Becoming a "professional lover" takes a lifetime and involves a lot of that "fourth ring." But the joy that it brings is so magnificent, the "meaningless noise" of mutually exploitative orgasms can't even be compared to it.

10. This all seems so heavy. Can't sex just be fun?

Sex *is* heavy. Like nothing else, it forces us to deal with the primordial "stuff" of life. The way we understand, think about, and live our sexuality has eternal consequences.

Because sex is literally the most creative force in the visible world (there's nothing greater than the power to cooperate with God in creating human life), when misused, it's also the most destructive. Sex confronts us with the most basic and powerful yearnings of our soul and forces us to grapple with the disparity between our highest aspirations and our basest inclinations. It forces us to choose between good and evil, between love and all that is opposed to love, between serving God and others (my spouse and our potential offspring) and simply serving myself.

John Paul II goes so far as to say that sexual union is a "test of life and death." When spouses become one flesh, he observes, "they find themselves in the situation in which the powers of good and evil fight and compete against each other."[9]

Holy Moses! This really *is* heavy. But there's a delightful paradox here. When we stop trying to run from how heavy it really is and instead choose to embrace the eternal magnitude of its importance, it no longer *weighs* on us. We experience what Christ meant when he said, "Take my yoke upon you ... and you will find rest for your souls. For my yoke is easy, and my burden is light" (Mt 11:29-30).

Living the truth about sex is intensely joyous. There simply is nothing that compares to the satisfaction of living in accord with the image in which we're made. There simply is nothing that compares to the joy of a husband and wife who embrace the truth—with all its risks, with all its ramifications, with all its responsibilities—when they embrace each other in the intimacy of their union.

Despite what the media encourages us to think, sex is not meant for our entertainment. Our genitals are not "sex toys." "Fun" is not the right word for marital union. Sublime ecstatic bliss is more like it. And if we understand that sacraments are foretastes of heaven, it's not merely a cliche to say that true, honest sex is an experience of heaven on earth.

If you want the greatest sex life possible, then give your sex, your life, and your sex life to Jesus Christ. If that sounds strange or makes you feel uncomfortable, then you've been overly influenced by too many people who have little to no clue about the meaning of life, the meaning of sex, and the meaning of Christ's mission in the world.

11. I've been married almost thirteen years. I know sex is supposed to be good, and even holy, but it still makes me feel dirty. What's wrong with me?

You're not alone. This rift between knowledge of how sex should be and how it's actually experienced is quite common, even among those who are striving to live the truth. Head knowledge is not enough by itself to undo the deep-seated and often unconscious attitudes we have about sex.

We need to go to their source and, with the help of God's grace, uproot them. Most often we'll find that the way we think and feel about sex as adults has much to do with the impressions we were given about our bodies and sex while growing up—from our parents, from siblings, from neighborhood friends, from exposure to pornography, from the media, from sexual experiences.

I'll often ask how many people in the audiences to whom I speak first learned about sex from their parents. I'd estimate that fewer than 5 percent of them raise their hands. This is tragic.

Children have a driving curiosity to know about their bodies, and about sex, even from an early age. If this curiosity is not properly directed and met in healthy and appropriate ways through open, honest, age-appropriate discussion in the home, sex becomes a big, dark, hidden "no-no," and children will inevitably seek to satisfy their curiosity in covert, distorted ways.

Speaking from my own experience growing up, I can still remember the first time I was exposed to pornography. I was about six or seven. I can conjure up those images in my mind to this day.

I remember kids telling "snake in the garden" and "Johnny Deeper" jokes that I didn't get. I remember a baby-sitter exposing himself to my brother and me and encouraging us to expose ourselves to him. I remember all kinds of lewd comments from older guys about girls and their body parts.

I remember "experimenting" with kids from the neighborhood and watching boys grabbing and probing girls through their swim suits in the public pool. I remember being shocked and mesmerized when an older kid told me in full detail what he did with a girl in his class. And I can still remember virtually everything he said.

These were my first impressions of sex. They affected me deeply. And this all happened before I reached puberty. I had no idea what to do with myself when my hormones really kicked in. A steady diet of pornography, masturbation, and adolescent "making out" sufficed until I started a four-year, sexually active dating relationship at age sixteen.

Why do I tell you all this? Because chances are you have similar memories from childhood and adolescence. Somebody needs to take the risk of talking about them. If we don't face the negative experiences that have formed us, we'll never be able to live in the freedom of the truth and to experience sex as it's meant to be.

Painful memories and wounds from distorted ways of thinking and relating don't just go away when you get married. Even people who really want to experience sex as God intends it are not uncommonly haunted by flashbacks of past sexual experiences right at the moment they're making love with their spouses. Many times people who have been exposed to pornography have those images parade through their minds at the least desirable moments: in times of prayer, at Mass (even while going to Communion), and while making love.

I speak honestly from my own experience also to demonstrate that when I speak of Christ's power to transform us, to heal our wounds and to save us from our sins, it's not just a nice concept in my head. It's something I've lived and continue every day to experience. *Christ, the Son of God, is real.*

He really became one of us. He really died for us and rose from the dead. He really came to restore God's original plan of life and love. He really redeemed us. He really can heal us. He really can grant us new life ... *if* we place our faith in him and *let* him.

My recommendation would be to look back into your own life. How did you first learn about sex? What were your impressions of your body as you went through puberty? Did others make fun of you? Were you ever exposed to pornography? Were you ever mistreated or abused sexually? Did you masturbate? Were you promiscuous as a teenager?

How did these experiences affect you? The purpose of such a reflection is not simply to dig up old dirt. The purpose is to bring the light of Christ into the dark places of our lives so that he can heal us.[10]

I remember at one point in my life writing on a piece of paper every sexual experience I'd ever had—all the junk that I had long tried to forget but couldn't—and going to a trusted priest to confess it. Afterward I lit the paper and watched it go up in flames. It was a true moment of healing for me and a real turning point in my life.

Furthermore, when Wendy and I arrived at the point in our relationship that we knew we would marry, I asked her forgiveness for not saving myself for her. What's that have to do with her, you ask? We're meant for sexual union with our spouse alone. Sex with others—even if it's long before you meet your spouse—is adultery "in advance." If we're brave enough to peel away all the layers of excuses we make for ourselves, we know this to be true.

There's a reason people are haunted by their pasts. There's a reason people feel uneasy at class reunions when they stand there with their spouse and see people they had sex with as a teenager. *Those experiences were not supposed to happen.*

Praise God that he forgives. Praise God that he restores. Praise God that he heals.

Don't sweep the past under the rug as if it were no big deal. Give it all to Christ and let it die with him on the cross. Seek the forgiveness of your spouse if you were unfaithful "in advance."

If you have flashbacks of past experiences, give them to Christ. Memories may remain, but Christ can remove their sting and teach you to use them as an opportunity to pray for the people you wronged and to forgive them for wronging you. This is the road to healing. This is the road, not only to knowing that sex is meant to be good and holy, but actually to *experiencing* it as such.

For many, like myself, it's a long road. It's a painful road. But it's not nearly as painful as the alternative. Where else can we go, Lord? You have the words of eternal life (see Jn 6:68).

Lord, you know me. Nothing about my life is hidden from you. You know all those things in my life that have drawn me away from the truth of your plan for my sexuality. Whether these were wrongs that I committed or wrongs committed against me, I give them all to you. Light of Christ, shine in the darkness. Truth of Christ, dispel all the lies.

Death of Christ, take all my sins. Resurrection of Christ, re-create me to know, live, and experience the goodness and holiness of my sexuality. Amen.

12. My mother said that when she was first married, a priest told her that she was obligated to "submit" to her husband's sexual needs upon request. What's up with that?

I don't doubt that your mother was told such a thing. The Church has long been fighting to correct errors that stem from misinterpreting St. Paul's admonition for wives to "submit to their husbands" (see chapter three, question 16). This is one such misinterpretation, and a very serious one at that. It all but blesses men's disordered desires to use their wives for their own sexual gratification.

It has *never* been the teaching of the Church that husbands are free to use their wives. On the contrary, it has been the constant teaching of the Church that husbands must love their wives as Christ loved the Church (see Eph 5:25). This includes what they do in the bedroom.

While they may not clearly recognize it, many wives experience a deep resentment toward their husbands that stems from being treated as a means to an orgasm. (Let's not think the proverbial "headache" is without cause.) Such hedonism on the part of the husband often produces a dreadful cycle that's devastating to a marriage: the husband desires sex for selfish purposes; his wife resists being used; the husband complains all the more that his wife doesn't "put out"; his wife withdraws all the more in the face of his complaints and demands.

This problem is further compounded by the fact that most men will point the finger of blame at their wives, when in reality, the lion's share of the problem is their own. Oh, the havoc sin has wrought on the original harmony of the sexual relationship.

It's a two-way street, of course. The balance of genuine love in intercourse must be maintained by both husband *and* wife. Still, as John Paul II puts it, "a special responsibility rests with the man, as if it depended more on him whether this balance is maintained or broken, or even—if already broken— reestablished."[11]

Husbands, if your wife consistently resists your desire for intercourse, my advice to you would be to look deeply into your own heart. Is your desire for sex a desire to make a gift of yourself to your bride and renew your marriage commitment? Or is it simply a desire to "relieve" yourself at her expense?

Allow your sexual desires to be crucified with Christ, so that they may be resurrected as the desire to love your bride as Christ loves his. If your wife knows in her soul that *this* is what you desire, she'll desire just as intensely to make a gift of herself to you, and there will be no more "headaches."

13. Didn't the Church used to teach that one of the specific purposes of marriage was the relief of sexual tension?

Traditional formulations of the Church taught that there are three ends of marriage: the primary end of *procreation*, the secondary end of *mutual help between spouses*, and the third end of *remedy for concupiscence*.[12] The Latin *remedium concupiscentiae* is translated by some as the "relief of concupiscence." This has led some to claim that marriage somehow provides a legitimate outlet for "relieving" sexual tension in the sense of *indulging* concupiscent desire.

Concupiscence, however, refers to our *disordered* sexual desires. By itself, concupiscence only leads toward the *use* of others for the sake of selfish gratification.[13] In no way does marriage justify this.

Quite the contrary. The grace of the sacrament of marriage, if we're open to it, provides a *remedy* for concupiscence. That is, it provides us with the power to experience a transformation in the very character of our sexual urges, so that such urges become the desire to love and not merely "relieve" ourselves as if we were scratching an itch. This understanding of the third end of marriage alone does justice to the dignity of the person.

We *know* that we're not meant to be used, especially by the ones who claim to love us the most. Far too many marriages lie in ruins because of the general mistrust, suspicion, and conflict between spouses that stem from treating sex as merely an opportunity to "relieve concupiscence."

14. Doesn't St. Paul justify relieving sexual tension when he says it's better to have sex in marriage than to burn with desire?

The passage you're referring to is actually directed to unmarried people whom St. Paul is advising to choose the celibate vocation. He says, "But if they cannot exercise self-control, they should marry. For it is better to marry than to be aflame with passion" (1 Cor 7:9).

Without getting involved in a thorough exegesis of St. Paul's words, we must understand that no Scripture verse stands alone. All verses and passages of Scripture must be interpreted in light of the entire Bible. When St. Paul talks about marrying, he's talking about the moral order. He's talking about husbands loving their wives "as Christ loved the Church," as he says in his Letter to the Ephesians (5:25). As much as love is better than lust, marriage is better than being "aflame with passion."[14]

Allow me to clarify another point. The "relief" of sexual tension is not wrong or bad in and of itself. God made sexual union to be an experience of heightened tension and climactic relief. Sharing the joy of this as husband and wife is an integral part of the sacramental symbol of married love. A "crisis in love" only arises when a spouse seeks that relief as *an end in itself* and treats his spouse as merely a *means to that end*.

15. Isn't there a fine line sometimes between love and self-seeking? It's not always easy to tell what my real motives are.

While at times we must admit it's quite clear whether we're being motivated by genuine love or by self-seeking, at other times it can be less so. We all have mixed motives. But recognizing them shouldn't be a source of discouragement. It's actually the first step in coming to a more mature evaluation of the inner movements of our hearts.

I don't hold myself out as one who loves his wife perfectly in this regard. I can only say from my own experience that the more I expose my heart to the light of Christ, the more I'm able to discern the purity, or lack thereof, of my motives. The human heart is a battlefield between love and lust. While the battle lessens the more we mature in the truth of God's plan for our sexuality, it never ceases entirely in this life.

The goal is simply to let the power of love hold sway over the pull of lust. Yes, at times the two can be confused. But with Christ's help we can acquire the courage necessary to be honest enough with ourselves to discern the difference.

"I Do ... Not"

Contraception

I call heaven and earth to witness against you this day, that I have set before you life and death, blessing and curse; therefore choose life.

The Word of the Lord[1]

I was seventeen years old and had been dating my girlfriend for about five months. She called me one Saturday afternoon to tell me her parents were going out for the evening. Tonight was the night.

On the way to her house, I stopped at a drugstore and, for the first time in my life, bought a box of condoms. As I placed the box on the cashier's counter, something inside me sank. Somehow I knew I was making a concrete decision to separate myself from God.

Not that I had been a saint up to that point. If I even had a relationship with God, it was hanging on by only a thread. But right then and there—in a Thrift Drug on Columbia Avenue in Lancaster, Pennsylvania—as I paid for those condoms, I severed the thread.

As I explained in the introduction, my unchaste behavior caught up with me in my college years, and I eventually came to agree with what the Church taught about sex—*except* on the issue of contraception. I had given up sex before marriage, but I thought when I got married I should be able to have sex with my wife whenever I wanted (without having to worry about raising fifteen kids). Besides, I thought, what was the difference between contraception and natural family planning if both are used to avoid pregnancy?

The more I grew in my faith as a Catholic, the more this issue became a real stumbling block. After all, one of the hallmarks of a Catholic is to believe and profess *all* that the Church believes and professes. Converts to the Church must specifically and publicly profess that they do. Cradle Catholics, on the other hand, can too easily fall into the hypocrisy of believing only what's comfortable. I knew that if I didn't come to terms with this "blasted" teaching, it would be more honest of me to be a Protestant. So I sought answers.

My search eventually led me to a book called *Catholic Sexual Ethics*.[2] It was the first thing I ever read that sensibly explained the Church's teaching. Again, something inside me sank. The Church had proved me wrong on so many things that I did *not* want to surrender my final "reserve." It took some more investigation, prayer, and humility before the scales fell off my eyes completely. Looking back, I marvel at how the issue that once severed my relationship with God (and the Church) was the same issue that brought me back—the *whole* way back.

Embracing this teaching changed the way I see, well, *everything*. The Church's teaching against contraception is where the rubber hits the road (pun intended). On this point we face a dramatic, though often undetected, clash between the forces of good and evil, between the fundamental human decision to love or not to love, to choose life or oppose it. Indeed, the entire Christian sexual ethic—everything discussed in this book—either stands or falls on this point. This is where spouses either choose to communicate God's life and love to each other and the world or choose to communicate, well, something else.

This is also *the* point of departure between Catholicism and popular culture. While our culture teaches that using contraception is the *responsible* thing to do, that it makes for better marriages and a better society, the Catholic Church stands as the lone voice saying it's *always* wrong and terribly damaging to marriage and society. Either popular culture has "lost its noggin," or the Catholic Church has.

If it's the Church that's gone batty, who'd want to be Catholic? On the other hand, if the Church is right, the twentieth-century promoters of contraception have pulled off the biggest snow job in history.

Lord, please help me, as I read this chapter, to open my heart to the full truth of your plan for sex and marriage. I don't want to be blinded by my pride. I don't want to be deceived by my own desires. I want to live the truth. Only the truth. Please Lord, if it's true that contraception is against your will, give me the grace to accept it, whatever the ramifications in my own life. I trust in you. Amen.

1. What in God's name could possibly be wrong with contraception?

Astute readers will recognize that everything we've discussed up to this point has paved the way to providing an adequate answer to this question. I'll begin answering it by once again stating the thesis of this book, and then posing a question of my own:

Sex is only sex to the extent that it participates in the "I do" of wedding vows. Is it ever permissible for a married couple to violate their wedding vows?

We can rant and rave and resist all we like, but an integral part of that "I do" is *openness to children*. Someone might respond: "A couple can be 'open to children' over the course of their marriage without *each* and *every* act of intercourse needing to be." But that makes as much sense as saying: "A couple can be 'faithful' to each other over the course of their marriage without *each* and *every* act of intercourse needing to be with each other." If we can recognize the inconsistency in claiming a commitment to fidelity ... *but not always*, we should be able to recognize the inconsistency of claiming a commitment to being open to children ... *but not always*.

Looking for a way out of the dilemma posed by this logic? You have a few choices:

Option 1: You can claim that sex doesn't have to participate in the "I do" of wedding vows at all. OK, then the logical conclusion is that it doesn't have to be between people who have exchanged wedding vows at all. In this view, sex has no real meaning whatsoever, other than the exchange, or even solitary experience, of physical pleasure.

This opens the door to the justification of any and every means to orgasm, whether by oneself, between two people, between any number of people (whether this is with the opposite sex or the same sex would be superfluous), or even with animals. This, unfortunately, is the way much of our contracepting culture already thinks.

Option 2: You can change the definition of marriage to exclude "openness to children" as an integral part of the commitment. OK, then *we* become the authors of marriage, rather than God, and the definition of marriage becomes completely arbitrary.

You want to have a "dissoluble marriage" just in case it doesn't work out? Sure, we can do that. You want to have an "open marriage" just in case you get bored with each other? Sure, we can do that. You want to "marry" your same-sex lover? Sure, we can do that.

After all, if marriage isn't intrinsically linked with procreation, why need it be between a man and a woman? This too, unfortunately, is the way much of our contracepting culture already thinks.

Option 3: You can claim that "openness to children" is part of the marriage commitment, but you need not always be faithful to it. We already discussed where this leads. It means you need not always be faithful to the commitments of fidelity or indissolubility, either. And this too, unfortunately, is the way much of our contracepting culture already thinks.

Marriage is all or nothing. Sex, as an expression of the marriage commitment, is also all or nothing. There is no avoiding the fact that an *intentionally sterilized* act of intercourse changes the "I do" of wedding vows to an "I do ... *not.*"

This "I do not" affects not only the commitment to being open to children. A closer look reveals that it also affects freedom, totality, and fidelity as well. Let's take a look at each of these again through the lens of contracepted intercourse.

Freedom. This truth may strike you as odd at first, but give it some time to sink in: *contraception was not invented to prevent pregnancy.* There already existed a perfectly safe, infallibly reliable way of doing that; it's called abstinence. Upon deeper reflection it becomes clear that contraception was invented *to indulge sexual instinct.* As the saying goes, necessity is the mother of invention. The necessity that mothered contraception was our "need" for sex.

"Sexual freedom," in the popular sense, means the license to have sex without ever having to say no (this is exactly what contraception affords). But only those who can say no to sex (only those who can abstain) demonstrate that when they say yes, they do so *freely.* Contraception, promoted in the name of "sexual freedom," actually fosters self-imposed slavery. It creates a culture of people unable to say no to their hormones.

Totality. As we noted in the last chapter, to the degree that we knowingly and intentionally reserve any part of ourselves from our spouse in the sexual act, we cannot speak of a *total* self-giving. This includes our fertility. Contracepted intercourse contradicts the "language of love" by saying, "I give you all of myself *except* my fertility. I receive all that you are *except* your fertility."

The choice to withhold one's fertility during intercourse, or to refuse to receive it as a gift in one's spouse, is a contradiction of the deepest essence of conjugal love right at the moment when it should find its most sincere expression. Precisely at marriage's "moment of truth," the truth is exchanged for a lie.[3]

Fidelity. Being faithful to one's spouse does not only mean refraining from adultery (in deed or in fantasy). It means living what you promised at the altar through thick and thin, no matter how difficult, no matter how challenging, no matter how much sacrifice is required. Couples who succumb to sterilizing their acts of intercourse have consciously or unconsciously decided that fidelity to their vows is too demanding. Consciously or unconsciously, they choose to be unfaithful to the promises they made at the altar.

Wedding vows are the expression of God's love on earth. When spouses contradict their vows through the language of their bodies, they contradict the very meaning of life—our call to image God by loving as he loves. So what in God's name could be wrong with contraception? It's precisely in *God's name*, in his nature as a life-giving Communion of Persons (the Trinity), that we find the most profound answer.

As we discussed in the first chapter, the Holy Spirit—as the very love shared between the Father and the Son—points, in some sense, to the fruitfulness of marital intercourse. I once gave a presentation at which a woman asked: "What if I want to have sex with my husband, but we don't want the Holy Spirit there?" I was taken aback. This is *precisely* why the Church teaches contraception is wrong, because this is *precisely* what a couple is saying when they contracept: "We don't want the Holy Spirit here."

Who's the Holy Spirit? *The Lord and Giver of Life* who proceeds from the Father and the Son. He's the very love and life of God!

When we understand the prophetic meaning of sexual union as a sacramental sign, the serious *contra*diction of *contra*ception becomes clear. Sex is meant to proclaim to the world that God is life-giving love. An intentionally sterilized act of intercourse proclaims the opposite: God *is not* life-giving love. Contraception turns sexual union from a prophetic act into blasphemy.

Furthermore, if the husband is to be a true symbol of Christ in the "one flesh" union, then he must speak the language of Christ: "This is my body which is given for you" (Lk 22:19). But a contracepted act of intercourse declares: "This is my body *not* given for you." In this sense, the contracepting husband acts not as Christ but as an anti-Christ.

And if the wife is to be a true symbol of the Church in the "one flesh" union, then she must speak the language of the Church (as modeled by Mary): "Let it be [done] to me according to your word" (Lk 1:38). But a contracepted act of intercourse declares: "Let it *not* be done to me according to your word." In this sense, the contracepting wife acts not as the Church but as an anti-Church.

An intentionally sterilized act of intercourse, then, rather than being an efficacious sign of Christ's one flesh union with the Church, is an efficacious *countersign* of this union (an anti-sacrament). Contraception turns sexual union from sacrament to sacrilege.

This, and nothing short of this, is what's at stake. *This* is why contraception is wrong, and not only wrong, but *grievously* wrong.

2. Are you saying couples who use contraception don't love each other?

They may love each other in many authentic ways. But despite any accompanying amount of sentiment, emotion, and feeling, an act of contracepted intercourse can *never* be an act of authentic love.

Love is not arbitrary. Love is not whatever we want it to be. Love is not merely an intense feeling or the sharing of pleasure. Love is to live according to the image in which we're made. Love is to give ourselves away freely, totally, faithfully, and fruitfully in imitation of Christ. Contracepted intercourse contradicts all of this.

3. So what the heck is a couple supposed to do, just have twelve kids? Gimme a break!

Let's think about it. Suppose there is a couple who have internalized what it means to renew their vows through intercourse and are determined *never* to violate those vows (as every married couple should be). Suppose also they have a just reason to space their children, or even not to have another baby at all. (We'll discuss what constitute "just reasons" in a subsequent question.) What could they possibly do that would not violate their vows?

Every time a couple chooses to have sex they *must* speak the "I do" of their vows. But couples aren't always obligated to have sex. In fact, throughout the course of a marriage there are many occasions when a couple might want to have sex but have good reason not to.

Perhaps one or the other spouse is sick. Perhaps the wife just gave birth. Perhaps the couple is staying with one of the in-laws and there are thin walls. Or perhaps they have a good reason not to have another baby. These are all good reasons *not* to have sex, even if they may *want* to.

So here's the answer to your question: If a couple had a good reason not to have another baby, and if they were firm in their resolve never to violate their marriage commitment (as every married couple should be), the only thing they could do would be to exercise their freedom to say no and abstain from sex. Human dignity and the meaning of sexual intercourse dictate that the only acceptable birth control is *self-control*.

Why do people spay or neuter their pets? Because animals can't say no to their urge to mate. But we *can*. If we can't, then we've stooped to the level of Fido and Fidette.

4. Are you saying a couple who needs to avoid pregnancy would have to abstain from sex until menopause in order not to violate their vows?

Let's think it through. Fidelity to the "I do" of the wedding vows means spouses must never do anything of their own will to sterilize any act of intercourse. Menopause actually gives us a good platform for discussion. If a couple past childbearing years chose to have sex, the lack of subsequent pregnancy would not be because of anything *they* did to sterilize the act. The lack of pregnancy would be the result of *God's* choice not to bring a new life into the world, as evidenced by his own design in the way he created the wife.

Well, it's also the result of God's design that women *within* their childbearing years are not always fertile. In fact, the large majority of the time, they're infertile.

Let's return to the couple who is determined never to violate their wedding vows. Out of respect for the meaning of sex, they abstain from intercourse because they have a just reason to avoid a pregnancy. Now let's suppose that on a given day of the wife's cycle they're able to determine that having sex would not result in pregnancy. Would they be doing anything wrong if they chose to have sex then?

If pregnancy did not result, would it be because *they* sterilized the act, or would it be because God chose not to bring a new life into the world as evidenced by the way he designed the wife's body?

This is the very principle of *natural family planning* (NFP). Couples who have been properly trained in modern methods of NFP can determine the fertile time of the wife's cycle with 99-percent accuracy.[4] If they have a just reason to avoid pregnancy, they choose to abstain from intercourse during that time. During the infertile phase of the cycle, if they so desire, they can choose to have intercourse without violating their marriage commitment in any way. The fact that pregnancy doesn't result from these acts of intercourse is *God's* doing, not *theirs*.

5. Isn't that splitting hairs? What's the big difference between sterilizing the act of intercourse yourself and just waiting until it's naturally infertile?

What's the big difference between an abortion and a miscarriage? What's the big difference between suicide and natural death? Like these examples, the difference between sterilizing an act of intercourse *yourself* and accepting the

God-given infertile time is one of cosmic dimensions.

As John Paul II once said: "Contraception is to be judged so profoundly unlawful as never to be, for any reason, justified. To think or to say the contrary is equal to maintaining that in human life, situations may arise in which it is lawful not to recognize God as God."[5]

This is the question at stake here: Are you free to take into your own hands the powers of life, or does that power belong to God and God alone? Think long and hard before you answer this question. How you do will determine your place in the cosmos.

6. Isn't refusing to have sex even more of a contradiction of your wedding vows than having protected sex?

I can't help but comment on this notion of "protected" sex. If your spouse poses some sort of threat to you, against which you must *protect* yourself by erecting a barrier, something's dreadfully wrong.

You can't separate your spouse from his or her fertility. The body expresses the person. To reject your spouse's fertility is to reject your spouse. True spousal love demands total surrender. There is no place here for "safety nets."

Refusing to have sex could well be a violation of your wedding vows if you were doing it out of spite for your spouse, out of hatred for children, or for some other negative reason. But spouses who mutually agree to abstain from intercourse because they have a *just reason* to avoid pregnancy are acting out of love and utter fidelity to their wedding vows. When spouses choose to "speak" (through intercourse), they must speak the truth. If they have a good reason not to "speak," it's good to remain silent. But nothing justifies speaking a lie by using "protection."

7. The Church's distinction between "natural" and "artificial" birth control makes no sense. Does this mean using polyester is immoral too?

Admittedly, it's difficult to see the important distinction between periodic abstinence and contraception when the emphasis is placed on "natural" versus "artificial" methods. There are lots of things we use that are artificial but not immoral, such as polyester. So why is artificial birth control any different?

Contrary to popular belief, the Church does not oppose artificial birth control *because* it's artificial. She opposes it because it's *contraceptive*. Contraception is the choice by any means *to impede the procreative potential of a given act of intercourse.* In other words, the contracepting couple chooses to engage in intercourse, and foreseeing that their act may result in a new life, they *intentionally* and *willfully* suppress their fertility.

This can be done by employing a large variety of artificial devices and hormones, or by sterilizing surgical procedures. It can also be done without employing anything artificial at all, such as in the practice of withdrawal (*coitus interruptus*). So in order to avoid a great deal of confusion, *contraception* is the best word to use when describing what the Church specifically opposes. "Artificial" really has nothing to do with it and is better left out of the discussion altogether.

Furthermore, the Church approves of NFP (when there is just reason to avoid pregnancy) not because it's "natural" as opposed to "artificial," but because *it's in no way contraceptive*. Never does the couple practicing NFP choose to impede the procreative potential of a given act of intercourse—ever. NFP is not "natural contraception." *It's not contraception at all.*

8. This is just another indication that the Catholic Church is opposed to modern progress and technology. If God gave us the intelligence to control our fertility, we should be able to use it.

As Pope Paul VI said in *Humanae Vitae*: "The Church is the first to praise and recommend the intervention of intelligence in a function which so closely associates the rational creature with his Creator; but she affirms that *this must be done with respect for the order established by God*."[6] Put another way: Yes, God gave us intelligence to regulate our fertility, and, yes, we should use it. But using our intelligence to act *against* God's design for our fertility is not intelligent at all.[7]

Allow me to demonstrate the concept this way. We'd all agree that the proper use of medicine and technology is to serve our health, to make our bodies work the way they're meant to work. For example, if medicine and technology can give sight to a blind man, that's a wonderful, intelligent use of it. But it would be a terrible abuse of medicine and technology *intentionally to blind someone* with perfectly functioning eyes. That would be an act of mutilation.

Well, it's no less a terrible abuse of medicine and technology, and no less a mutilation, *to sterilize someone intentionally*. If someone is fertile, that means his or her body is functioning the way it's meant to function.

As philosophy professor Janet Smith points out, we take pills when we're sick. We have surgery to cure maladies and disease. Fertility is not a sickness. Fertility is not a disease. Infertility is the malady that needs to be cured.[8] The only intelligent thing to do when there is honest need to regulate fertility is to come to understand God's design for fertility and work with it. That's what NFP is all about.

9. I *still* don't see the big difference between NFP and contraception.

Do you *want* to see the difference? Many people don't, because somewhere they intuit that it would demand not just a change of behavior in the bedroom but the transformation of their entire worldview. If that's what you're sensing—you're right.

As we hinted in question 5, the way we understand the order of the universe shifts in one of two irreconcilable directions on this point. Either God is God, and we trust his ordering of the universe, or we're trying to be God and control things ourselves. My advice: Let God be God.

There's nothing to fear. Trusting him is only threatening if he's a tyrant. He's not. He's perfect love. Let go. Let him in. Trust him.

If you're open to seeing the difference, I think the following analogy will help. Suppose there were a religious person, a nonreligious person, and an antireligious person walking past a church. What might each do?

Let's say the religious person goes inside and prays, the nonreligious person walks by and does nothing, and the antireligious person goes inside the church and desecrates it. (I'm framing an analogy, of course, but these are reasonable behaviors to expect.) Which of these three persons did something that is always, under every circumstance, wrong? The last, of course.

Husbands and wives are called to be *procreative*. If they have a good reason to avoid pregnancy, they are free to be *non-procreative*. But it's a contradiction of the deepest essence of the sacrament of marriage to be *anti-procreative*.

The analogy is even more profound than you may think. According to Ephesians chapter 5, the wife is a sacramental sign of the Church. As exemplified in the Virgin Mary, woman's womb has truly become the temple of God. If the husband enters this "church," he must pray for God's will to be done. He may have a good reason not to enter the "church." But it would be a grievous sacrilege to enter the church and desecrate it by sterilizing her womb.

Here's another analogy.[9] Most engaged couples come to realize in planning their weddings that there are people they know whom, with good reason, they can't invite to the wedding. The proper thing to do is simply not to send them an invitation. Can you imagine sending them a "*dis*-invitation"? "We are getting married on June 21, but we do *not* want you to be there. Please do not come." That would be an obvious breach of the relationship.

This is what married couples are doing to God when they contracept. By engaging in intercourse, they are sending God an invitation to join them in bringing about his most creative act, but when God opens the invitation, it says in bold letters: **"Do Not Come. We Don't Want You Here."** On the other hand, couples who abstain from intercourse to avoid pregnancy are simply not sending an invitation to God. If the couple has a good reason to avoid a pregnancy, God can understand that. There's no breach of relationship.

10. I was always taught that morality is evaluated by intention. Don't couples using NFP and those using contraception have the same intention?

We must be careful to distinguish between *present* and *further* intentions (means and ends). They may have the same *further* intention—to avoid pregnancy for just reasons. But their *present* intentions (the means by which they intend to achieve their common end) are very different. The NFP couple *intends to abstain* from fertile intercourse. The contracepting couple *intends to sterilize* fertile intercourse. These are different intentions altogether.

Take, for example, two students who both have the further intention of getting good grades. With that goal in mind, one intends to study hard, and the other intends to cheat on every test. The end never justifies the means.

11. Where does the Bible say contraception is wrong?

Where does the Bible say that it's wrong to take your neighbor's arm and run it through a meat grinder? It doesn't. But it does say we're called to love our neighbor. Sensible people will draw the conclusion that love of neighbor excludes making hamburger out of his arm.

Nowhere does the Bible say, "Thou shalt not use contraception." But it does say we're created in the image and likeness of God as male and female (see Gn 1:27). It does say "be fruitful and multiply" (Gn 1:28). It does say that God slew Onan for "spilling his seed on the ground" (Gn 38:9-10).[10]

Christ himself taught, in reference to the two becoming "one flesh," that we must not separate what God has joined (see Mt 19:6), and God's the One who joined sex and babies, isn't he? Ephesians chapter 5 very clearly calls husbands to love their wives as Christ loves the Church. Would Christ ever intentionally sterilize his love?

From beginning to end the Scriptures call us to receive God's love, to love as God loves, and to choose life. Sexual union is perhaps the most pointed opportunity for us to accept this call or to reject it. It's through sexual union that the uncreated love of God penetrates the created world to commune with the love of husband and wife in bringing about the most stunning event in the universe: the creation of a new human person.

Contracepted sex says: "We don't want to receive God's love. We don't want to love as God loves. We don't want to choose life." Is *that* biblical?

12. So what would be just reasons for a married couple to use NFP to avoid pregnancy?

First we need to look at the general disposition a couple has toward children. A contracepting culture tends to see children as a burden to be resisted, rather than a gift to be welcomed; an obstacle to material wealth, rather than a contribution to family health; a drain on the world's resources, rather than a benefit to society.[11] Within this milieu, couples often enter marriage with an approach to children that assumes they won't have them *unless* or *until* they want them. After the allotted two, it seems a couple would have to find justification for having any more.

Without thinking anything of it, couples who take this approach simply look for the most expedient way to carry out their plan. From this perspective, NFP is just seen as another choice on the long list of methods of avoiding "unwanted" children, and a very undesirable method at that. While it's just as effective at avoiding pregnancy as any contraceptive method, it takes far too much sacrifice to practice.

But suppose such a couple did use NFP. Their negative mentality toward children is already contrary to what they pledged at the altar. Regardless of the fact that they're not intentionally sterilizing their acts of intercourse, they would be guilty of violating their vows "in their hearts."

To return to the wedding invitation analogy, it's not that such a couple is sending a "dis-invitation" to God but that their withholding an invitation is not based on a just reason. It's based on an attitude that God's presence in their union would not be welcome.

This is still an obvious breach of relationship. (How would you feel if a close friend didn't invite you to his wedding without good reason?) So before all else, we need a deep conversion of our hearts to the meaning of sex and the true blessing of children in order to understand the just use of NFP in a marriage.

Every married couple is called to "be fruitful and multiply" (Gn 1:28). This is the starting point. Children are not something tacked on to married love but are the crowning glory of married love. Thus, instead of avoiding children, the general disposition should be one of receiving children as they come, unless a couple have a good reason not to.

The Church readily recognizes, especially in our day and age, that many couples *do* have good reason not to receive children as they come at certain times of their married life. The Second Vatican Council offers the following guidelines for spouses in planning their family size: "[Spouses should] thoughtfully take into account both their own welfare and that of their children, those already born, and those that the future may bring. For this account-ing they need to reckon with both the material and the spiritual conditions of the times as well as their state in life. Finally, they should consult the inter-ests of the family group, of temporal society, and of the Church herself. The parents themselves and no one else should ultimately make this judgement in the sight of God."[12]

The *Catechism* states that it's the duty of parents to "make certain that their desire [to space births] is not motivated by selfishness but is in conform-ity with the generosity appropriate to responsible parenthood."[13]

Let's return, once again, to the couple that truly understand the meaning of sex. They have a proper attitude toward children. God is always welcome in their sexual union. Yet they've discerned before God, based on the above prin-ciples, that they should avoid another pregnancy, at least for the time being.

Such a couple are not concerned with the amount of sacrifice necessary to be faithful to their vows, so they learn how to use NFP and abstain from sex-ual activity during the fertile time of the cycle. That is, with good reasons, they refrain from inviting God to create a new life. Such a couple act justly, responsibly, and in full accord with the commitment they made at the altar.

13. We already have five kids. It is my decision—and should be my decision—to make sure I don't get pregnant again. The pill is what my husband and I have decided is best for our family. It's none of the Church's business. If the Church really had great love for families, it would allow them to choose the birth control method that works best for them instead of trying to make them feel guilty about the method they choose.

Let me caution you that there are only three ways "to make sure you don't get pregnant again." The first is to abstain from sex altogether until you are post-menopause. If you want to continue having sex, the only other options are complete removal of your ovaries or complete removal of your husband's testicles. No method of birth control, except for these three, is 100-percent effective. Even with vasectomy or tubal ligation, you can't be sure that you won't get pregnant again if you and your husband continue to have sex.

As a mother of five, you can no doubt relate to the following analogy. If you had a fifteen-year-old daughter who wanted to go to an unsupervised party where you knew there would be a lot of drinking, drugs, and promiscuous sex going on, I would imagine that out of love for her you would tell her it's not good to go. Your daughter might not see your love for her in this. In fact, she might scoff at your supposed love and say, "If you really had such great love for me, you would realize that my going to this party is none of your business, and you would allow me to decide for myself what is best instead of making me feel guilty for wanting to go."

As a mother, you're able to see something that your daughter, for whatever reason (maturity level, peer pressure, misinformation, or whatever), is unable to see. Going to this party, no matter what your daughter "believes," is *not* good for her.

In a similar way, we who have been baptized into the Catholic Church are all her sons and daughters. The Church, in a real sense, is our mother. Sadly, even as adults, we don't always know what's best for us. The Church, as a loving mother should, seeks to guide us.

We can resist all we like, just as a child might. But guided by Christ himself, the Church knows the right path for us. It's the narrow path. It's the path on which few are willing to travel (see Mt 7:13-14). It's the path of following in the footsteps of Christ and living according to his wisdom and not our own "beliefs." It's the path of trusting that God has our best interests in mind even when we don't understand.

In the end, what you choose to do is indeed your decision and can be only your decision. The Church cannot, and never claims to, make decisions for others. As John Paul II himself said, the Church "does not impose her teaching, but feels an urgent need to propose it to everyone without fear and indeed with great confidence and hope although she knows that [it] includes the subject of the Cross. But it is only through the cross that the family can attain the fullness of its being and the perfection of its love."[14]

14. When it comes to birth control, the Catholic Church has lost touch with the needs of real people. No other church teaches that birth control is wrong. The Catholic Church loses all credibility right here.

If the Church is wrong about this issue, I would agree. She is "out of touch" and loses all credibility right here. But if the Church is right about contraception, then it's the rest of the world that's "out of touch," and the Catholic Church *gains* all credibility right here.

Contraception is nothing new. In fact, one of the hallmarks of the early Christians that distinguished them from their pagan contemporaries was their refusal to diminish their fertility with the linen condoms, potions, and pessaries (obstructions placed in the vagina) of their day. Until 1930 *every* Christian denomination was unanimous in its condemnation of contraception.

That year, however, the Anglican Church made history as the first Christian body to break with this teaching. At the time, Catholic, Protestant, and even non-Christian voices predicted that acceptance of contraception would logically lead to societal chaos, starting with a dramatic rise in marital breakdown and divorce. You might be surprised to read what several prominent thinkers of the early twentieth century had to say about contraception.[15]

U.S. president Theodore Roosevelt, for example, condemned contraception as "the one sin for which the penalty is national death, race death; a sin for which there is no atonement." Sigmund Freud, the founder of modern psychoanalysis and an atheist, observed: "The abandonment of the reproductive function is the common feature of all perversions. We actually describe a sexual activity as perverse if it has given up the aim of reproduction and pursues the attainment of pleasure as an aim independent of it."

Mohandas Gandhi, the famous Indian nationalist leader and a Hindu, insisted that contraceptive methods are "like putting a premium on vice. They make men and women reckless." He predicted that "nature is relentless and will have full revenge for any such violation of her laws. Moral results can only be produced by moral restraints.... If [contraceptive] methods become the order of the day, nothing but moral degradation can be the result.... As it is, man has sufficiently degraded woman for his lust, and [contraception], no matter how well meaning the advocates may be, will still further degrade her."

T.S. Eliot, the celebrated British poet and literary critic, insisted that by accepting contraception, "the world is trying the experiment of attempting to form a civilized, but non-Christian mentality. The experiment will fail; but we must be very patient in waiting its collapse; meanwhile redeeming the time so that the Faith may be preserved alive through the dark ages before us; to renew and rebuild civilization and save the world from suicide."[16]

When a committee of the Federal Council of Churches in America issued a report that suggested following the lead of the Anglican Church, *The Washington Post* published a stinging editorial with the following prophetic statement: "Carried to its logical conclusions, the committee's report if carried into effect would sound the death knell of marriage as a holy institution by establishing degrading practices which would encourage indiscriminate immorality. The suggestion that the use of legalized contraceptives would be 'careful and restrained' is preposterous."[17]

Wise men and women have always recognized the power of the sexual urge to orient, or disorient, not only individuals but entire societies. But in the midst of chaos as we now are, it can be hard to see the forest for the trees.

What's the connection between contraception and the breakdown of marriage and society? I offer the following as a plausible, but admittedly simplified, explanation.

People are often tempted to do things they shouldn't do. Many deterrents within nature itself and within a society help to curb these temptations and maintain order. For example, what would happen to the crime rate in a given society if jail terms suddenly ceased? Let's apply the same logic to errant sexual behavior and see what happens.

People throughout history have been tempted to commit adultery. It's nothing new. But one of the main deterrents to succumbing to the temptation has been the fear of an unwanted pregnancy.

Hmm ... What would happen if this natural deterrent were taken away through the widespread availability and cultural acceptance of contraception? Not in every marriage, of course, but in a given population, incidents of infidelity would be sure to rise. And what's one of the main causes of divorce? Adultery.

But let's continue with this scenario. Certainly throughout history young people have been tempted to have sex before marriage. Yet one of the main deterrents to succumbing to the temptation has been the fear of unwanted pregnancy. Once again, what would happen if this natural deterrent were taken away through contraception? Not in the case of every hormone-laden young person, but in a given population, incidents of premarital sex would be sure to rise. And premarital sex, as noted in chapter four, is also a key predictor of future divorce.

It gets worse. Since no method of contraception is ever 100-percent effective, an increase in adultery and premarital sex in a given population will inevitably lead to an increase in "unwanted pregnancies." Abortion logically follows (see question 16 for more discussion of this subject).

Not everyone will resort to abortion, of course. Some will offer their children up for adoption. Other mothers will keep them. Hence the number of children who grow up without a father (which has already been increased by the rise in divorce) will be compounded.

As numerous studies (and common sense) indicate, the chances dramatically increase that these "fatherless" children will grow up in poverty; be abused; have emotional, psychological, and behavioral disorders; suffer poor health; drop out of school; engage in premarital sex; obtain abortions; do drugs; commit violent crimes; and end up in jail. All these social ills compound exponentially from generation to generation since "fatherless" children are also much more likely to have out-of-wedlock births and, if they marry at all, to divorce.[18]

Welcome to the societal chaos in which we now live. It couldn't be more serious. As journalist Philip Lawler has observed: "[T]he public consequences of 'private' sexual behavior now threaten to destroy American society. In the past thirty-five years the federal government has spent four trillion dollars—that is $4,000,000,000,000—on a variety of social programs designed to remedy ills which can be attributed, directly or indirectly, to the misuse of human sexuality."[19]

These ills were predicted by wise men and women who understood the power of contraception to alter the course of society by altering people's approach to human life at its source. If marriage is the fundamental cell of society, sexual union is the fountainhead of culture. Oriented toward love and life, it builds a culture of love and life. Oriented *against* love and life, it builds a culture of utility and death.

If nothing governs life at its source, then nothing governs life. A contracepting culture is a culture without a future. It's a culture, as T.S. Elliot and Theodore Roosevelt understood, that's committing suicide.

The twentieth century witnessed every major Protestant denomination shift from condemning contraception, not only to accepting it, but oftentimes advocating it. The Catholic Church alone—withstanding unimaginable global pressure—has stood firm. Even staunch Protestant leaders, when they wake up to the evils of contraception (as more and more are), marvel at the courage of the Catholic Church. As one Evangelical Lutheran put it: "That a Roman pontiff would lead the opposition—often painfully alone—to contraception at the end of the twentieth century is no small irony. Perhaps the Catholic hierarchical model, reserving final decisions on matters of faith and morals to a bishop whom Catholics believe is the successor of Peter, has proved more resilient in the face of modernity than the Protestant reliance on individual conscience and democratic church governance."[20]

So, is the Catholic Church out of touch with the needs of real people, or is the prevailing contraceptive culture? Real people need the truth. Real people need to know the good news of our creation in the image of God and our call to love as Christ loves. The Catholic Church proposes this good news to the world. It's our choice whether to embrace it or reject it.

15. You're overlooking a host of benefits. Contraception has helped liberate women, brought more equality between the sexes, and freed married couples to enjoy sex more by relieving the fear of unwanted pregnancies. How can that be wrong?

What does it mean for women to be liberated? What *is* equality between the sexes? What *is* the joy of sex? Let's look briefly at each and see what contraception has done.

Women's liberation. History has demonstrated what the Book of Genesis foretold: men will dominate women (see Gn 3:16). Women *should* seek liberation from this domination. But if the real problem behind women's oppression is men's failure to treat them properly as persons, contraception is a sure way to keep women in chains. Remove the possibility of pregnancy, and you simply foster men's tendencies to treat women not as persons to love but as things to use for their own pleasure and to discard when they're through.

The first feminist leaders of the nineteenth century recognized this. Women such as Elizabeth Cady Stanton, Victoria Woodhull, and Dr. Elizabeth Blackwell all spoke out against contraception, seeing it as still further degradation of women since it gave men license to indulge their passions without consequence.[21] In a calamitous break with the wisdom of their predecessors, twentieth-century feminists would actually come to believe that contraception was the key to women's liberation.[22]

Only after the casualties of the sexual revolution have some modern feminists awakened to the delusion. Germain Greer, for example, who once encouraged her followers to revel in the "liberties" afforded them by contraception, now laments that "contraceptive technology, instead of liberating women, has turned them into geishas [Japanese term for "call girls"] who risk health and fertility in order to be readily available for meaningless sex."[23]

In keeping with the foresight of the first feminists, Pope Paul VI predicted that contraception would result in the further degradation of women in his encyclical *Humanae Vitae*.[24] Gandhi predicted the same. History has proved all of them right.

Equality between the sexes. Our equal dignity as men and women is founded on God's creating us in his image as male and female. But equal in dignity does not mean *sameness*. It's precisely in the beauty of sexual *difference* that we discover our complementary and equally dignified personhood.

Contraception is actually opposed to woman's equality. It seeks to turn her into someone God didn't make her to be—that is, the kind of person who can have sex without getting pregnant—in order to be "equal" to (read "the same as") men.

Think about it. If women have to alter themselves in order to claim "equality," then their equality is nothing but a sham created by technology, not by God. Men will only treat women as equal in dignity when they come to appreciate woman's unique giftedness as God made her to be. Contraception seeks to eradicate that uniqueness.

The joy of sex. The true joy of sex is loving as God loves in a free, total, faithful surrender of self that's open to life. From this perspective, couples who use contraception don't enjoy sex at all. They may enjoy the pleasure of orgasm exchange, but they don't enjoy sex.

Technically speaking, a couple that contracept aren't even having sex. They don't want to have sex. They're afraid of what sex *is*. They're afraid of the demands of love. If they weren't, they wouldn't be using contraception.

Contraception doesn't relieve people of their fears. It demonstrates how afraid they actually are. Only true love can cast out fear (see 1 Jn 4:18). Only true love can bring true joy. If all you want is the pleasure of orgasm, it's safer just to masturbate.

Could there be some genuinely good things that have come from contraception? Yes. But trying to justify contraception by pointing them out would be like trying to justify the Nazi Holocaust by pointing to the fact that it created jobs. You can create jobs in morally acceptable ways.

Similarly, any genuine good that has come from contraception can be brought about in other, morally acceptable ways. We may never do evil so that good may result (see Rom 3:8).

16. How can the Church not recognize the contradiction of being against both contraception and abortion? Abortions will continue as long as there are unwanted pregnancies.

Pope John Paul II addresses this issue in his encyclical *Evangelium Vitae*: "It is frequently asserted that *contraception*, if made safe and available to all, is the most effective remedy against abortion. The Catholic Church is then accused of actually promoting abortion, because she obstinately continues to teach the moral unlawfulness of contraception. When looked at carefully, this objection is clearly unfounded. It may be that many people use contraception with the view to excluding the subsequent temptation of abortion. But the negative values inherent in the 'contraceptive mentality' ... are such that they in fact strengthen this temptation when an unwanted life is conceived."[25]

By using contraception, a couple set their will *against* the conception of a child. If their contraception fails (as it can and often does), then they're stuck with a child growing in the womb that they didn't bargain for, that they weren't prepared for, *that they didn't want.*

What do they do now? Even a cursory look at the data indicates that in every country that has accepted contraception, abortions have multiplied, not diminished. The United States Supreme Court itself recognizes the inherent connection: "In some critical respects abortion is of the same character as the decision to use contraception.... For two decades of economic and social developments, people have organized intimate relationships and made choices that define their views of themselves and their places in society, in reliance on the availability of abortion in the event that contraception should fail."[26]

Thus contraception has afforded the grand illusion that we can sever the inherent connection between sex and babies. People then say the strangest things, such as: "I got pregnant by accident."

Whoa! As Janet Smith is fond of pointing out, if you were having sex and you got pregnant, it doesn't mean something went *wrong*, it means something went *right*. Even doctors, when confronted with their contracepting yet pregnant patients, will ask: "How did this happen?" We really have a problem on our hands when even the medical community has forgotten where babies come from.[27]

"Unwanted babies" are the result of people having sex without being open to children. Pregnancy comes to be seen as a disease—contraception being the preventative medicine, and abortion being the cure. Trying to solve the abortion problem with contraception is like trying to put out a fire by dousing it with gasoline! Only by restoring the full truth about the goodness, the beauty, and the demands of sexual love can we prevent "unwanted babies" and their murder.

There's yet a further connection between contraception and abortion that cannot go unmentioned. Many people are unaware that the IUD, the pill, and other hormonal contraceptives such as Depo-Provera™ and Norplant™ can at times act not to prevent conception but to abort a newly conceived human being.

Chances are you know someone who got pregnant while on the pill. So obviously the pill doesn't always prevent ovulation. In fact, hormonal contraceptives are believed to have two "backup" mechanisms, should ovulation not be prevented: (1) They prevent sperm from reaching the egg by changing the consistency of the cervical mucus; and (2) they change the lining of the uterus so that a newly conceived child cannot implant in the uterine wall and dies. (It's believed that the IUD works almost exclusively this way).[28]

Of course, few doctors are telling their patients this. In fact, there has been a push in the medical community to redefine the beginning of pregnancy as the moment of implantation rather than the moment of conception in order to disguise the abortifacient mechanism of these "contraceptives."[29]

17. What if you're on the pill for medical reasons? Is that still wrong?

First let me state the moral principle involved, then I'll address the pill specifically. As Pope Paul VI said in *Humanae Vitae*: "The Church ... does not at all consider illicit the use of those therapeutic means truly necessary to cure diseases of the organism, even if an impediment to procreation, which may be foreseen, should result therefrom, provided such impediment is not, for whatever motive, directly willed."[30]

Suppose a woman had a hysterectomy to remove a cancerous uterus. Subsequent sexual acts would obviously be sterile, but the intention of the operation was to remove her cancer, not to sterilize her. (Note: A medical reason to avoid pregnancy does *not* justify sterilization.) The fact that she is now sterile is an unfortunate but unintended consequence of a medically necessary procedure.

Taking the pill for medical reasons would be similarly acceptable, but for the fact that the pill is a potential abortifacient. If there were absolutely no medical alternatives for a married woman on the pill for therapeutic reasons, she and her husband would have to abstain from sex *completely* in order to avoid the risk of aborting their children. The good news is, there are many medical alternatives to the pill. The Pope Paul VI Institute for the Study of Human Reproduction specializes in such alternative treatments.[31]

18. NFP isn't 100-percent effective either. So even if everybody used NFP as the Church says, there would still be the temptation to abort.

This would be the case only if those who were using NFP already had the wrong attitude in their hearts toward children. Let's return, once again, to the wedding invitation analogy (see questions 9 and 12 above). How would you feel if you sent a "dis-invitation" to someone, but that person had the nerve to show up? You'd be upset, wouldn't you? You'd want to tell that person to get out. This is precisely why the contraceptive mentality leads to abortion.

Furthermore, even if a couple wouldn't resort to abortion, we can see how the contraceptive mentality leads to a resentment toward children and all that they demand of their parents. Back to the "dis-invited" wedding guest. Suppose you didn't have the nerve to kick him out. Still, you'd resent his presence. And you'd be all the more indignant if he made demands on you at the reception. Quite simply, the lifelong responsibilities of parenthood are not what contracepting couples bargain for.

The mentality of those who make responsible use of NFP is totally different. Suppose you sent a wedding invitation to someone whom you already knew couldn't make it to your wedding. How would you feel if he had a change of plans and unexpectedly showed up? You might be surprised, but you wouldn't want to kick him out. After all, you'd invited him to come. If you did want to kick him out, that would demonstrate that your invitation was insincere in the first place.

This is analogous to the NFP couple having sex during the infertile time. They send an invitation to God saying he's free to create a new life if he so desires, but they are nearly certain he won't. If God has a "change of plans," you might hear the couple speaking of a "surprise pregnancy," but you'll never hear them speaking of an "unwanted pregnancy." If they do, then it will show that their invitation to God was insincere in the first place.

To put it another way, couples who make responsible use of NFP know what the bargain is and embrace it. If God unexpectedly chooses to create a new life, every diaper change, every sleepless night—in short, every parental sacrifice—becomes a continuation of the *yes* they uttered in the ecstasy of that life-giving embrace.

19. NFP couples must have lots of surprises, then. The chart in my doctor's office says natural methods are only 80-percent effective at avoiding pregnancy.

The 80-percent figure often quoted in medical literature is based on studies of people who simply say they use some "natural method of birth control." This could include people who use the older "rhythm method," or those who simply guess when they are or are not fertile, or those who have actually been educated to use a modern method of NFP. It may also include people who knowingly fudge on the time of abstinence.

Grouping this lot together, an 80-percent figure is probably accurate. But if you take the group of people who have been properly educated in modern methods of NFP and who are motivated to follow the rules, the effectiveness rate jumps to 99 percent, as numerous studies indicate.[32]

20. I thought NFP *was* the rhythm method. What's the difference?

This is a common misunderstanding. The older rhythm method, popularized by Catholics in the mid-twentieth century, predicted the probable time of fertility in a given month based on the length of past cycles. Thus it was not very effective for women with irregular cycles. Nor was there any way of determining when fertility would return after childbirth or while breast-feeding.

Progress in understanding the role of cervical mucus throughout the 1950s and 60s led to the development of modern methods of NFP. These are not based on the probability of fertility, but rather on the readily observable signs of fertility and infertility in each cycle (primarily cervical mucus, but also temperature, changes in the cervix, and other signs). Thus, any woman can use modern methods of NFP successfully, even if she has irregular cycles, is breast-feeding, or is premenopausal.

21. So how long do you have to abstain with NFP if you want to avoid pregnancy?

Usually no more than twenty-seven days per cycle. Just kidding. In all honesty, only about seven to twelve days per cycle. Periods of abstinence may be longer during times of irregular fertility such as after childbirth and premenopause.

22. There's nothing "natural" about abstaining from sex when you're married. Seems to me it could even harm a marriage.

Abstinence could harm a marriage if it were done for the wrong reasons. But when a couple choose to abstain from sex out of fidelity to their wedding vows, it only serves to strengthen their marriage. We can see this by looking at each of the promises of marriage again through the lens of NFP.

Freedom. Practicing NFP puts a couple's freedom to the test. Even if they find it difficult, periods of abstinence, when chosen in fidelity to the marriage commitment, cannot help but strengthen both husband and wife in the virtue of self-mastery, so essential to the freedom of authentic conjugal love.

Totality. Practicing NFP promotes total self-giving by respecting the total person. The refusal to erect physical or chemical barriers creates an atmosphere that enables spouses to let go of emotional barriers as well. Each spouse knows he or she is respected by the other. Each spouse sees the other's genuine love in his or her willingness to sacrifice. Thus spouses establish a mutual trust that enables them, when they do have sex, to surrender totally to each other without fear.

Fidelity. Fidelity to the marriage commitment is the *raison d'être* of NFP.

Such couples demonstrate their fidelity to their vows no matter how difficult, no matter how challenging, no matter how much sacrifice is required. Do you think a couple that have learned to say no to sex within marriage when appropriate would have any trouble saying no to temptations for sex outside marriage when presented?

Openness to children. Maintaining fidelity to this promise is, of course, the hallmark of NFP. When couples who practice NFP choose to have sex, they always leave the possibility of pregnancy in the hands of God. The Holy Spirit is welcome in their bedroom. The bond of love that unites the Trinity becomes the very same bond that unites them.

There's no question that the periodic abstinence required by NFP can be difficult. But as the Fathers of the Second Vatican Council remind us, "a true contradiction cannot exist between the divine laws pertaining to the transmission of life and those pertaining to authentic conjugal love."[33] Practicing NFP takes self-control, trust in one's spouse, trust in God, honest and open communication, and willingness to sacrifice for each other. But love isn't harmed by these things. Love *is* these things.

Since practicing NFP fosters the very virtues that make for a successful marriage, it shouldn't surprise us that while—across the board—Catholics have about the same divorce rate as everybody else, surveys indicate a virtually nonexistent divorce rate among NFP users.[34] Far from damaging marriage, practicing NFP is marriage insurance.

23. What's acceptable regarding marital intimacy during the time of abstinence?

Many of the principles that should guide a couple's expressions of affection when they're abstaining during the fertile time have already been discussed. For example, couples shouldn't be seeking the pleasure of climax apart from an act of intercourse. But this doesn't mean they should take a "hands off" approach, either.

Practicing NFP is a wonderful way for spouses to learn that intimate signs of affection don't always need to lead to intercourse.[35] Kissing, embracing, caressing—such signs of affection are all good in themselves and shouldn't be withheld because a couple doesn't intend to have sex. We're called to freedom. If a couple can't express genuine affection for one another without being tempted to masturbate, then something's amiss. On the other hand, couples need to know their own limits (these vary greatly from couple to couple) and discuss them openly and honestly to avoid "pushing the envelope" toward climax.

24. I accept what the Church teaches, but my husband insists that we use contraception. What should I do?

Continue patiently to lead him to the truth and meaning of your marriage by your own example of Christlike love. Above all, pray for him. The ultimate goal of your marriage is to lead each other to heaven.[36]

Know that your suffering in this situation is not in vain. Offer it to Christ in intercession for your husband's change of heart. Expect miracles. I've seen them happen. If God can change *my* heart on this issue, he can change anybody's heart.

In the meantime, don't cooperate in the sin of your husband by directly assisting in the contraceptive behavior. For example, don't take the pill or insert a diaphragm for his sake. If he knows where you stand and still withdraws during intercourse, or even forces the use of a condom, then he alone is responsible for the contraceptive behavior.

You also have the option of refraining from intercourse as long as your husband insists on contracepting. Various consequences of this choice need to be weighed, but forcing a spouse to cooperate in objectively sinful behavior is abusive, and you are in no way obligated to submit to it. Out of concern for yourself, and for him, you may want to let him know you aren't available to be treated as a thing for his sexual "relief," all the while loving your husband and helping him to experience a change of heart.

25. I had my tubes tied. Now I regret it. What should I do?

First things first. If you haven't already received the sacrament of reconciliation, find a priest who understands and upholds the Church's teaching, and go. Trust in the Lord's mercy. He heals. He forgives. In addition, you and your husband should seek a fresh start by asking each other's forgiveness for being unfaithful to the commitments you made at the altar.

There are many women (and men who have had vasectomies) in the same boat with you. Some of them don't find peace until they have their sterilizations reversed. If you have the means and you're not a high-risk patient, that's an option I'd certainly recommend.[37] Since reversal surgery can be costly (insurance rarely pays for it), and any surgery involves some amount of risk, it isn't a moral necessity. Nevertheless, genuine contrition and repentance *are* a moral necessity.

One way of showing that repentance is by abstaining from sex for a set time each month as if you were practicing NFP. Many people in your situation find that approach very beneficial as they seek to grow more and more in a true understanding of the meaning of marital love. You could also devote time to spreading the Church's teaching on these issues as a way of preventing others from making the same mistakes.

Above all, trust in God's merciful love. *Nothing* we've done in our lives is beyond the scope of the redemption Christ won for us.

26. We've been contracepting for years. We've never heard any of this stuff. What should we do?

Again, first things first. If you haven't already received the sacrament of reconciliation, find a priest who understands and upholds the Church's teaching, and go. Trust in the Lord's mercy. He heals. He forgives. Seek each other's forgiveness as well.

Then, by all means (even if you're skeptical) *take an NFP class!* Countless couples who have experienced the damaging effects of contraception on their marriage can speak to the healing effects of learning and practicing NFP.[38]

"I Do," But Not As God Intends

Reproductive Technologies

Life teaches us, in effect, that love—married love—is the founda-tion stone of all life.

Pope John Paul II[1]

"W ill we still need to have sex?" This was the first question posed by *Time* Magazine in a series entitled "Beyond 2000: 100 Questions for the New Century." "Birds do it. Bees do it. But we may no longer have to do it—except for the fun of it," declared the subtitle of this alarming article. And without a second thought, under an eerie picture of miniature human beings being spawned in test tubes, a caption proclaimed: "The link between sex and pro-creation, already tenuous, could be severed."[2]

Welcome to Aldous Huxley's *Brave New World*.

This should horrify us. The link between sex and procreation holds the dig-nity of human life in place. Sever it, and human life is automatically cheap-ened. Sever it, and human beings come to be treated no longer as persons to love but as things to use.

On the one hand, this utilitarian approach leads to the destruction of human beings when it's supposed that they get in the way of our happiness—both at the beginning of life (abortion) and at the end (euthanasia). On the other hand, it leads to the technological production of human beings when it's supposed that they can bring about our happiness. In either case, human life is not respected for its own sake but is treated as a thing to be acquired or dis-carded according to personal preference.

Infertility is a real problem, one that has skyrocketed in the last thirty years in developed countries.[3] In response, an entire, ever expanding, and little regulated "reproductive technologies industry" has emerged. While the desire to overcome infertility is certainly legitimate, there are still important moral considerations to take into account.

As good as the desire for children is in itself, it doesn't justify any and every means of "getting" a child. For example, kidnapping another person's baby is wrong no matter how desperately a couple want children. So also, as the Church teaches, is manufacturing children through technological procedures. In both cases, we're dealing with a *good end* (the desire for children) but a *bad means*.

The pain and even anguish of infertile couples mustn't be dismissed. But much more is at stake in the laboratory generation of human life than is first apparent. The Church's teaching against certain reproductive technologies raises many pressing questions and objections. Before I address them, I'd suggest giving some serious thought both to the following seven questions and to the implications of your answers.

Are we the masters of human life?

Is a child a gift from God?

Can a gift be demanded?

Do couples have a right to children at any cost?

Do couples have a "right" to children at all?

Are we free to determine what is good and evil?

Are God's commandments meant to bring us happiness or keep us from it?

1. The Church is so pro-family and pro-child. It makes sense that the Church would be against technologies that impede procreation, but what could possibly be wrong with technologies that are intended to bring life into the world?

It does seem contradictory at first. Upon further investigation, however, it becomes evident that the Church would be contradicting herself if she *didn't* teach the immorality of some techniques of generating life. The Church's teaching on reproductive technologies is simply the "flip side" of her teaching on birth control.[4] While contraceptive methods of birth control divorce sex from babies, many reproductive technologies divorce babies from sex. Steadfast consistency in upholding the meaning of love, life, and marriage—the meaning of being created male and female in the image of God—demands that the link between sex and babies, babies and sex, *never* be divorced, regardless of circumstance or motives.

The Church's basic moral principle concerning reproductive technologies is this: If a given medical intervention *assists* the marital embrace at achieving its natural end, it can be morally acceptable, even praiseworthy. But if it *replaces* the marital embrace as the means by which the child is conceived, it's not in keeping with God's intention for human life.[5] Separating conception from the loving embrace of husband and wife not only provokes many further evils, but—even if these are avoided—it remains contrary to the dignity of the child, the dignity of the spouses and their relationship, and our status as creatures. Let's look at each of these issues.

Provocation of further evils. As Christ said, you can judge a tree by its fruit (see Mt 7:17-20). Separating conception from the marital embrace doesn't *necessarily* entail the following evils, but more often than not, it leads to them in practice: masturbation as a means of obtaining sperm; production of "excess" human lives that are either destroyed through abortion (euphemistically referred to as "selective reduction"), frozen for later "use," or intentionally farmed for medical experimentation; a "eugenic mentality" that discriminates between human beings, not treating all with equal care and dignity; the trafficking of gametes (both sperm and ova) and frozen embryos for use by others; insemination of unmarried women and, therefore, all the evils associated with "fatherless" children outlined in the previous chapter.

The dignity of the child. While there are many acts through which a child *can* be conceived (the marital embrace, an act of rape, fornication, adultery, incest, various technological procedures), only one is in keeping with the dignity of the child. As chapter one explained in some detail, humanity's great dignity is found in our imaging of God. Love is our origin, vocation, and end. Thus human dignity demands that a child be conceived through that act of love that images God. This is marital love, and its defining expression is the embrace of husband and wife in "one flesh."

From the moment of conception, children deserve the respect we owe all persons. They are equal in dignity with their parents. They are created for their own sake, to be received unconditionally as gifts from God. To desire a child not as the fruit of marital love but as the end result of a technological procedure, is to treat the child as a *product* to obtain, rather than a *person* to love. For those involved, this creates—consciously or unconsciously, subtly or not so subtly—a depersonalized orientation toward the child.

Products are subject to quality control. When you spend top dollar for a new TV, you want it in mint condition. You don't care about the TV you pulled out of the box for its own sake. You want one that works. If it's defective, you'll take it back for a refund or exchange it for another one.

Similarly, the temptation is all too real for a couple paying thousands (even tens of thousands) of dollars for these procedures to want a "refund" or an "exchange" if their "product" is defective. The mentality of the approach leads people to want not the particular baby conceived for his or her own sake but rather babies in "mint condition," even babies "made to order": this sex, that eye color, this skin tone, that stature. In fact, if the baby is deformed or doesn't otherwise meet the couple's (or the doctor's) specifications, he or she is often "scrapped," and the procedure is started over.

I don't mean to imply that every couple who pay for these procedures stoop to this level. The temptation to apply "quality controls" *can* be resisted. But a depersonalizing mind-set is built into the very nature of the procedure.

The only way to ensure that the dignity of *every* child is respected is to ensure that spouses understand and live the full meaning of sex and never seek children apart from their union. No child, with whatever "defects" might occur, could ever be unwanted or unloved if he or she were the fruit of the parents' union that imaged God. Unconditional love begets unconditional love.

The dignity of the spouses and their relationship. The Congregation for the Doctrine of the Faith has observed that if the generation of human life is to respect not only the child but also the parents and the dignity of their relationship, it "must be the fruit and the sign of the mutual self-giving of the spouses, of their love and of their fidelity."[6] In other words, in keeping with what we've discussed throughout this book, the generation of human life must be the fruit of the "I do" of wedding vows expressed through sexual intercourse.

The technological generation of human life is simply *not marital*. The child is not the fruit of his parents' wedding vows "made flesh." The child is the product of a technological procedure performed by a third party apart from their union altogether. As moral theologian William E. May has noted: "Spouses can no more delegate to others the privilege they have of begetting human life than they can delegate to others the right they have to engage in the marital act."[7] The fact that the gametes being used by the technician may be those of a husband and wife is superfluous to the manner of the child's conception.

So yet again, spouses who employ these procedures violate, consciously or unconsciously, the "I do" of their marriage commitment.[8] While spouses may desire to express their "openness to children" through recourse to these procedures, at best they're saying, "I do, *but not as God intends.*" Acting contrary to God's plan for marriage and procreation is utterly incompatible with the marriage commitment, even if it's done with the "best of intentions."

Furthermore, numerous couples can attest to the depersonalizing effects of subjecting themselves to numerous tests and repeated procedures that treat their sex cells as "raw material" to be mined for the production of a child. Being artificially inseminated by a doctor with a long syringe isn't on any woman's top ten list of most dignified experiences, either. Some may claim that it was all worth it when their "miracle child" is born. But the underlying realization that their child is a "miracle of science" rather than a miracle of their own marital union cannot help but serve to unravel the basic psychology of family relationships on which spouses and children alike depend for equilibrium.

The marital embrace is not simply the biological transmission of gametes. If such were the case, it would be much more expedient for couples wanting to conceive to employ *in vitro* techniques rather than leave it up to biological "chance." The marital embrace is a profoundly personal, sacramental, physical, and spiritual reality. To divorce human conception from this sublime union shows a lack of understanding and respect for the "language of the body" and the deepest essence of married love. It depersonalizes all involved.

Our status as creatures. God alone is, as we affirm in the Nicene Creed, the "Lord and Giver of life." Spouses have the distinct privilege of cooperating with God in procreating children, but as creatures themselves, they aren't the masters of life. They're only the servants of God's design.

Technological fertilization, on the contrary, as the Congregation for the Doctrine of the Faith has noted, "entrusts the life and identity of the embryo into the power of doctors and biologists and establishes the domination of technology over the origin and destiny of the human person."[9] Spouses and technicians thereby set themselves up as *operators* instead of *cooperators*, *creators* instead of *procreators*. They deny their status as creatures and make themselves "like God" (see Gn 3:5).

God created sexual union, as we've been saying throughout, to be a sacramental symbol of his own life and love and of our union with Christ. Seeking human life apart from sexual union is also symbolic. It symbolizes rejection of our union with God: the desire to have life *without* God or, at least, apart from his design for us. As the *Catechism* says, when we prefer our own designs to God's, we thereby scorn him. When we choose ourselves against the requirements of our creaturely status, we act against our own good.[10]

2. Are you saying children conceived from these technologies aren't created by God, or aren't made in his image?

There's not a single person on the planet who would exist if God didn't will for him to exist. As soon as sperm meets egg, even if it's in a petri dish, God is there to create an immortal soul. But even though God wills for technologically conceived children to exist, and allows them to come to be in this way, it doesn't mean that God wills for us to use these technologies.

Similarly, God wills the existence of children conceived through acts of rape and incest (if he didn't, they wouldn't exist), but this doesn't mean he wills for us to engage in rape and incest. While all such children themselves bear the image of God and are to be loved and treated like any other human being, none were conceived by an act that images God. This is and always will remain an injustice to them.

Here we find ourselves confronted by the mystery of God's interaction with our freedom. God doesn't intervene in our decisions to act unwisely. To do so would be to deny us our freedom. (What a tremendous gift and what a tremendous responsibility our freedom is.)

It's God's nature, however, to bring good out of our wrong choices, even the greatest good possible—a new human person. Does this mean we should act badly in order for good to result? If we do, according to St. Paul, our condemnation is deserved (see Rom 3:8).

3. We play God every time we have surgery or take medicine. What's the difference with these reproductive technologies?

Fitness, health, and life are written into our very being as part of God's original plan for us. Sickness, disease, and death are all a result of the corruption caused by original sin. God allows them, but he does not *will* them *per se*. So assuming that all the means employed are licit in themselves, we act in complete accord with God's plan when we use medicine and technology to save a life or restore health.

In these cases, we're not acting as the masters of human life but as the stewards that God made us to be. Similarly, when we assist the marital embrace in achieving its natural end, we act as stewards in restoring God's design. But as soon as we *replace* God's design and seek to "force" a conception, we cross the line from steward to master, from being creature to playing God.

4. Didn't you say that infertility is a disease (see chapter six, question 8)? According to your own words, doesn't this imply that it would be a good use of medicine and technology to overcome it?

Yes, infertility is a disease, or perhaps more aptly, a disability. Seeking ways to cure it is a praiseworthy service to the many married couples who suffer greatly because of it. But there are limits to what can be done.

The same statement from *Humanae Vitae* quoted in chapter six is applicable here as well: "The Church is the first to praise and recommend the intervention of intelligence in a function which so closely associates the rational creature with his Creator; but she affirms that *this must be done with respect for the order established by God.*"[11] If we use our intelligence to *assist* the marital embrace at achieving its natural end, then we act as stewards of God's design, respecting the order he established. But as soon as we *replace* the marital embrace as the means of conception, we act outside the scope of God's order.

In fact, only by *assisting* the marital embrace can we speak of a true *cure* for infertility. Replacing intercourse in no way cures the couple's malady. It only bypasses it.

God's order isn't arbitrary. It's meant for our good, for our benefit. It's a mystery that God allows some fornicators and adulterers who don't even want children to conceive, while at the same time he allows loving husbands and wives to suffer with infertility. Who can fathom that? But both situations offer an opportunity for those involved to turn to God and abandon themselves to him.

God's ways are not our ways. As high as the heavens are above the earth, so high are God's ways above ours (see Is 55:9). Trust him. This is what Christ teaches us. He himself felt abandoned by God on the cross (see Mk 15:34). But even in this darkest hour, he trusted. And as his resurrection attests, his trust was not in vain.

Lord, help me to trust you with my life and all the circumstances of it, even—and especially—when I don't understand. Give me the grace to believe in your promise to bring good out of every suffering and disappointment that you allow in my life. Amen.

5. I understand that children are supposed to be the fruit of their parents' love. But children conceived from these technologies can be the fruit of their parents' love on a spiritual level.

It's true that love is spiritual, for God, who is pure Spirit, *is* love (see 1 Jn 4:8). But human beings are not pure spirits. We are *body-persons* (see chapter three, question 10; chapter five, question 6, for a more complete discussion of this issue). It's in and through our *bodies* that we image God and share his love with others. This is nowhere better exemplified than in the expression of love unique to marriage: the union of husband and wife in one *flesh.*

Spouses who seek such technological procedures may do so because they want to have a child to love. And they may certainly love the child once he or she has been produced. Nevertheless, as much as we may like to think it's possible, no amount of mental gymnastics or wishing can transport the couple's "spiritual love" outside of their bodies and onto the procedure of the doctor or scientist. The fact remains that such a child's origin is not the incarnational love of the parents, but rather the end result of depersonalized technological procedures.

6. Why is adoption acceptable? Adopted children aren't the fruit of the couple's sexual union.

Adoption isn't only acceptable. It's laudable. While it's true that an adopted child isn't the fruit of the couple's union, providing a loving home for a child who *already exists* is completely different from manipulating a child into existence.

One is an act of love. The other isn't. Couples who are unable to conceive should prayerfully consider whether God is calling them to open their homes to children in need of adoption.

7. My brother's wife is unable to have children. They've asked me if I'd be willing to be a surrogate mother. I love my brother and want to help. What's wrong with that?

Love *always* chooses the good and helps others do the same. Genuine love for your brother is incompatible with a willingness to carry his child. Not only is this a grave distortion of the natural order of family relationships, but it would also necessitate *in vitro* fertilization. This is wrong for all the reasons already mentioned.

The best way for you to help your brother would be to encourage him to embrace the truth of God's plan for sex and procreation in his marriage. If that means he'll never have a child that's biologically his own, God will give him the grace to accept that. He need only open his heart to it.

8. Didn't God call us to have dominion over nature?

God called us to subdue the earth and have dominion over the animals (see Gn 1:28). As long as we're responsible stewards, we're free to manipulate creation for our benefit. There's nothing wrong, for example, with artificially inseminating cattle. They're not called to love in God's image. But this rightful dominion does *not* extend over human beings.

Nor can the body be considered part of the realm of "subhuman" nature over which we do have dominion. As John Paul II warned in his *Letter to Families*, "When the human body, considered apart from spirit and thought, comes to be used as raw material in the same way that the bodies of animals are used ... we will inevitably arrive at a dreadful ethical defeat."[12]

9. Lots of unmarried women have a sincere desire for children. These technologies can fulfill their hopes. What's wrong with that?

These technologies are wrong in and of themselves for all the reasons already mentioned. But there are even further considerations in the case of using them to impregnate unmarried women.

Many women make the heroic effort of raising children when the father is absent due to no fault of their own. They're to be commended for their dedication and sacrifices. But there's an enormous difference between a single mother who *regrets* the absence of her children's father and a single mother who *chooses* to deny her child this irreplaceable relationship. To desire a child in this way can only be self-serving.

Perhaps it's easy to think, "So-and-so's children turned out fine without a father. It's not so terrible." But no child who has grown up without a father is without wounds. Only through the secure and recognized relationship of children to their mother *and father* are they able to discover their own identity and achieve their own proper human development.[13] What does it do to a child's sense of self when all he or she can possibly know about his or her father is that he masturbated at a sperm bank for money?

10. I can see why single people may not have a right to children. But it's terribly cruel for the Church to deny a loving married couple the right to have a child when they so desperately want one.

A married couple's desire for children couldn't be more natural. The Church is the first to recognize and share in the painful trial of couples who find they are unable to conceive. It's natural to want to alleviate a couple's sufferings by granting them their legitimate aspirations whenever possible. But as we noted previously, we find ourselves on very dangerous ground when we let mere sympathy guide our moral decisions, especially when such decisions concern the very life and destiny of another human being.

The Church is the defender of people's legitimate rights. She never denies them. Spouses, however, cannot claim a legitimate *right* to children.[14]

Children are a gift given by God. No couple is entitled to them, nor can they be demanded. The commitment spouses make at the altar to "receive children lovingly from God" reflects this reality.

Spouses have the right only to engage in the marital embrace and pray for God's will to be done.[15] They are certainly free to make the conditions for conception as optimum as possible, but whether or not a child results from their self-giving must be left in God's hands. The Church's teaching on the intrinsic immorality of technological fertilization actually upholds the only legitimate human right in question: the right of the child "to be the fruit of the specific act of the conjugal love of his parents."[16]

11. So what's a couple supposed to do if they can't have kids but really want them—just suffer?

They can do a number of things. First and foremost, they should take a natural family planning class. NFP is true family planning. Pinpointing the fertile time of the cycle can obviously help a couple achieve a pregnancy as well as help them avoid one.

Believe it or not, most doctors are not even trained to recognize the signs of fertility and what they mean. Many a couple who have had difficulty conceiving have realized after learning NFP that it was simply a problem of timing.[17]

Generally speaking, even if couples are certain they're having intercourse during the fertile time, there's only about a one-in-three chance of achieving pregnancy. Couples aren't considered in need of medical assistance for infertility unless they're certain they've had intercourse during the fertile time for six months without conceiving. For those who are engaging in random intercourse without knowledge of the fertile time, it's twelve months.

At this stage of the process, those intent on conceiving should seek medical advice. For anyone in this situation, I highly recommend calling the Pope Paul VI Institute for the Study of Human Reproduction.[18] The staff work on a national basis and specialize in helping couples in ways that are truly therapeutic—that is, in ways that seek to cure the given malady rather than bypass it, thus allowing couples to conceive naturally through their conjugal union. Their approach is much more successful (and usually much less expensive) than methods of technological reproduction.

Still, there is a certain percentage of couples who, after exhausting all legitimate solutions, find they are still unable to conceive. The Congregation for the Doctrine of the Faith has this to say about their plight: "Couples who find themselves in this sad situation are called to find in it an opportunity for sharing in a particular way in the Lord's Cross, the source of spiritual fruitfulness.

Sterile couples must not forget [as John Paul II has observed] that 'even when procreation is not possible, conjugal life does not for this reason lose its value. Physical sterility in fact can be for spouses the occasion for other important service to the life of the human person, for example, adoption, various forms of educational work, and assistance to other families and to poor or handicapped children.'"[19]

The sufferings of infertile couples need *not* be in vain. Borrowing words from my own archbishop, Charles Chaput: "Suffering can bend and break us. But it can also *break us open* to become the persons God intended us to be. It depends on what we do with the pain. If we offer it back to God, he will use it to do great things in us and through us, because suffering is fertile."[20]

Yes, suffering is spiritually *fertile*. These are not empty words of consolation. Through Christ's example, we know these words are "spirit and life" (see Jn 6:63).

12. My doctor wants to do a sperm count to see if I'm the cause of our infertility. Is it OK for me to masturbate to supply the semen?

No, it's not. Remember that the end does not justify the means. The intention to masturbate is wrong regardless of the further intention for which it's done. It is possible, however, to obtain sperm morally through an act of intercourse in which you use what's known as a "perforated condom." Some sperm are released into your wife's vagina (so as not to be contraceptive), and some sperm are retained for analysis.[21]

13. Sometimes there can be a fine line between assisting and replacing the marital act. How can you tell the difference?

Most of the time it's quite obvious. Either the child is conceived from intercourse, or he or she is not. But you're right: Some procedures may involve an act of intercourse, yet it's difficult to know whether the child actually results from that act.

One such procedure is known as GIFT (Gamete Intra-Fallopian Transfer). Husband and wife engage in intercourse using a perforated condom (as described above). Technicians then place sperm retained in the condom in a small tube separated from the wife's surgically removed ovum by an air bubble. The contents of the tube are then injected into the wife's body with the hope that fertilization will occur.

If a child is conceived, the question remains: Is he or she the fruit of the marital embrace or the end result of a technological procedure? The Church hasn't to date made any definitive pronouncement, and theologians disagree.

It seems to me, however, that assistance or replacement of the marital act can be determined by asking the following question: Is the marital act an essential precursor to the meeting of sperm and egg, or could fertilization have happened just as well without it? It seems that in the GIFT technique, marital intercourse is not essential, since sperm could have just as easily been obtained through masturbation. Furthermore, the sperm that eventually fertilizes the egg was not even ejaculated into the wife's body but was intentionally withheld for the procedure.

That being said, I think it's safer to avoid GIFT and other techniques of fertilization in which intercourse is treated only as a "moral way" to obtain sperm.

14. We have a beautiful daughter conceived by artificial insemination. We prayed and prayed that God would bless us with a child, and we believe he did. We couldn't imagine life without her. I refuse to believe that what we did was wrong.

Admitting that what you did was wrong does not mean you must conclude that your daughter herself is "wrong." Nor does it mean that your daughter's existence is not a gift from God. As we stated earlier, your daughter would not and could not exist if God did not will for her to exist. She *is* a blessing from God.

God is always looking for "excuses" to bless us and show us his love, even (believe it or not) when we act outside his plan. Still, although a great blessing has come from it, the manner of her conception remains an injustice to her. Honesty, and the good of all concerned, calls for that recognition.

I might compare your situation to that of some friends I know. They have a ten-year-old son. They love him very, very much and, like you, couldn't imagine life without him. They know he's a blessing from God in their lives. But they've been married less than ten years themselves. He was conceived out of wedlock.

What they did—having sex outside of marriage—was wrong, seriously wrong. To pretend otherwise would be an additional injustice to all involved, especially their son. They know someday he'll do the math, and they'll all talk about it. He'll probably have some issues to work through, but the situation isn't beyond the scope of God's redeeming love. Nothing is, except the pride that refuses to admit when we've been wrong.

15. We knew the Church taught it was wrong but never understood why until now. We wanted a baby so badly, and through *in vitro* we now have twins. Is God angry with us? What should we do?

First of all, continue to love your twins and be grateful to God for them. They are a sign that God loves you and trusted you with these precious lives, even when you turned from his will to your own. What a loving, merciful God we have. We shouldn't presume on his mercy, but when we express true sorrow for our wrongdoing, we should certainly trust in his mercy.

Find a priest who understands these issues, and go to confession. When the priest absolves you of your sins, know that Christ himself is forgiving you.

Is God angry with you? Not in the way we typically understand anger. He's "angry" in the sense that any father would be pained by seeing his children make poor decisions. But he's not vindictive. God's anger and his love, his justice and his mercy, are one and the same reality.

Like the father in the story of the prodigal son, he runs to embrace us and welcome us home even when we're still far off in our journey back to him (see Lk 15:11-32). Yes, God is running to you. Run to him.

Eight

When Saying "I Do" Is Impossible

Same-Sex Attraction

If we don't live the sexual differences correctly that distinguish man and woman and call them to unite, we will not be capable of understanding the difference that distinguishes man and God, and constitutes a primordial call to union. Thus, we may fall into the despair of a life separated from others and from the Other, that is, God.

Stanislaw Grygiel[1]

The rise of homosexuality as a publicly accepted "alternative lifestyle" is yet another by-product of a culture that has severed sex from its inherent link with procreation. Even gay activists such as Andrew Sullivan recognize this. Making his case for same-sex marriage, he argues: "The heterosexuality of marriage is intrinsic only if it's understood to be intrinsically procreative; but that definition ... has long been abandoned by Western society."[2] Long abandoned by society (thanks to contraception)—but firmly maintained by the Catholic Church.

The Church's teaching is unwaveringly consistent. For those who have followed the course we've charted throughout this book, the logic behind Catholic teaching on the intrinsic immorality of homosexual behavior is probably already clear. To leave it at that, however, simply doesn't do justice to the issue.[3] The Church's teaching on homosexuality raises pressing questions and objections.

This is not just an abstract issue. Real men and women are involved here. Real lives are affected. According to Catholic writer David Morrison, author of the book *Beyond Gay*, if you include the loved ones of those with same-sex attraction, there are approximately twelve million Americans intimately affected by this concern. "That means," he writes, "twelve million people for whom every charge and countercharge, every misunderstanding, every mis-communication, mischaracterization, and slur can strike at the heart of who they consider themselves to be or the kind of life one of their loved ones is try-ing to build. No wonder questions of same-sex attraction, gay or lesbian rights, and same-sex marriage or adoption have the explosive emotional force they do."[4]

I'm one of those twelve million. More than one person I love has struggled or does struggle with homosexual attraction. I myself went through a painful period in my teenage years of questioning my masculine identity.

One of my high school religion teachers did a room full of insecure pubes-cent boys a terrible injustice when she told us we couldn't possibly know whether we were "gay" until we were at least twenty-five. We all looked around the room and tried to boost our macho facades with a deep-throated "Yeah, right, not me." But underneath, I was struck with mortal fear that I might wake up one day and discover I was "gay." This fear, coupled with a memory I had desperately tried to repress of "experimenting" with a friend from school when I was about ten, would eventually play a key role in leading me to my knees seeking from God what it means to be a man (see the Introduction to this book).

If you're a man, God created you to be a man. If you're a woman, God cre-ated you to be a woman. There is inherent *meaning* to your sex.

No one need be afraid to look deeply and honestly into his or her soul and admit the distortions and confusions found there, *whatever* they might be. We *all* have them. But no confusion, no distortion of our identity as men and women, goes deeper than the cross of Christ. The only tragedy is refusing to label them as distortions and seeking to "normalize" them for fear of the cross.

Lord, you created me to be a man [woman] for a reason. Show me the meaning of my sexual identity, and give me the grace not to fear admitting how far I may be from it. You know me better than I know myself. You know my struggles, my deepest fears, my wounds, my sins. Lead me, one step at a time, closer to your plan for creating me to be a man [woman] in your own image. I surrender all that I am to you and trust you to bring to completion the work you've begun in me. Amen.

1. My priest said the Church teaches it's OK to be gay, just not to act on it. Is that true? Seems like a contradiction to me.

It seems this priest is referring to the wise distinction the Church makes between the homosexual *tendency* and homosexual *behavior.* Few people who identify themselves as homosexuals would ever claim they *chose* to be so. Since same-sex attraction is not freely chosen, it's not a matter of sin itself. But this doesn't mean it's a good thing to act on it.

There's no contradiction here. Alcoholics have a disordered desire for booze. Overeaters have a disordered desire for food. These desires themselves aren't a matter of sin, but this doesn't make it good to act on them.

Still, this priest's statement needs to be clarified. First of all, as understood in the secular world, when someone labels himself as "gay" (or herself as "lesbian"), it most often implies, "This is the way I was born. I will always be this way, and I plan to live this way." Despite what all the pro-gay propaganda would have us believe, no one *is* gay. That is, no one is *ontologically* (in his or her very being) oriented toward the same sex.

Because of the fallen world in which we live, same-sex attraction is a reality that many people must face, but these attractions can never define *who* a person *is* in the essence of his or her identity. It's true that a person's identity can't be separated from his or her sexuality. But *sexual identity* refers to being created either as a *male* or a *female*.

The meaning of our sexual identity is inseparable from our complementary call to life-giving communion in the image of God. Original sin has obscured this call in each of us to some degree or other. But it hasn't changed the fact that this is who God created us to be.

As we've discussed throughout the book, the body is the revelation of the person. Because of the body's nuptial meaning, we can conclude that every human person is ontologically oriented toward the *opposite sex*. This is plainly obvious from the way God created our bodies.

If someone experiences a strong attraction toward the same sex, this is more properly described as a *disorientation*, since it departs from the natural, God-given complementarity of the sexes. Again, since people generally "discover" they are attracted to the same sex rather than "choosing" to be so, there's no moral fault connected with this disorientation. Even so, it's very important to realize that same-sex attraction is itself, as the Church describes it, an "objective disorder," in that it departs from the original *order* established by God.[5]

Returning to the original question, we can see that it's misleading to say the Church teaches it's "OK to be gay." Saying something is not sinful in itself isn't the same as saying it's "OK." This can lead to the erroneous conclusion that homosexual attraction is neutral or even good. If that were the case, it *would* be contradictory to claim that acting on such desires is immoral. But such attraction cannot be neutral, much less good, because it's ordered toward an intrinsic moral evil—homosexual behavior.[6]

Fallen human beings are attracted to many things that are morally evil; homosexual behavior is only one such thing on a very long list. As noted earlier, that attraction is called *concupiscence*. It comes from sin and entices to sin but isn't sinful in itself. It's merely a given of the fallen human condition.

But precisely because concupiscence comes from sin and entices us to it, it's not "OK." We're called to overcome it—whether it manifests itself in same-sex attractions, or in a disordered attraction to the opposite sex, or in a disordered desire for food or drink.[7]

Like everyone else, those who experience homosexual attractions are called to live chastely; that is, they're called to experience the redemption of their sexuality through an ever-deepening appropriation of Christ's work in their lives (see chapter four, question 12). To be sure, same-sex attractions can be a particularly difficult cross to bear. But God's liberating grace is ever present to help us live according to his original plan of love. This is why the Church's teaching about sex, including her teaching on homosexuality, is good news.

2. What could possibly be wrong with two people of the same sex loving each other? If love is of God, it can't be wrong.

You're right. It's never wrong to love. We run into a problem, however, when we project our understanding of love onto God. It goes the other way. *God is love* (1 Jn 4:16). If we are truly to love others, regardless of their sex, then our love must conform to God. It must be "in his image." Otherwise, it's simply not love.

Unfortunately, the English language doesn't distinguish between different kinds of love. A man's relationship with his wife, his mother, his best friend, even with his favorite dessert, are all described by the word "love." All of these loves (except "love" for apple pie, although that, too, shares in God's appreciation for the goodness of all that he has created) can image God, but each does so in different ways.

Sexual or erotic love is a very particular way of imaging God. The project of this book has been to demonstrate that we can only image God sexually by expressing the "I do" of wedding vows: the free commitment to indissolubility, fidelity, and openness to children. And it's simply *impossible* for two people of the same sex to express this commitment to each other.

Another way of saying this is that it's simply impossible for two people of the same sex to have sex. Whatever homosexual behavior may consist of, it *is not* and *cannot* be sexual union. Sexual union is brought about by the inseminating union of genitals. A man's genitals cannot unite with another man's genitals, nor a woman's with another woman's. It's simply impossible.

Yet again we're confronted by the "problem" of our bodies. Any attempt to divorce our souls from the fundamental orientation of our bodies (yes, our genitals) is to embrace the ancient heresy of *dualism*. Those who seek to justify homosexual behavior are *ipso facto* guilty of splitting body and soul.

The dissenting Catholic group called Dignity, for example, shows the root of its error when it seeks to undermine the procreative meaning of sexual expression with insinuating questions such as this: "Is the biological or the personal the key aspect of sex among human beings?"[8] The biological *is* personal. It's *the body* that shows us who we are and defines our call to sexual love. There's no way around it. Divorce love from the truth of the body and, at best, you're left with a shadow of love; at worst, its antithesis.

There is absolutely nothing wrong with two persons of the same sex loving each other. But erotic love between two members of the same sex is an oxymoron. Love always chooses the good of the person loved. Love never does wrong or entices another to do so. Members of the same sex who truly love one another will never seek to engage in erotic behavior with each other specifically *because* of their love.

3. What's the difference between the sexual union of a married couple known to be sterile and the behavior of homosexuals? Neither one is "open to children."

As we discussed earlier, remaining open to life means never intentionally rendering a sexual act infertile or seeking climax in a way not designed for the generation of life. Even if a married couple is known to be sterile through no fault of their own, their sexual union is still a genital union. Their sexual union is still the kind of union that God has intended for the procreation of children.

On the other hand, it's physically impossible for two members of the same sex to engage in a genital union (a union of genitals). It's physically impossible for two members of the same sex to engage in the kind of act that God has designed for the generation of life.

Even so, your question is on to something. There's little moral difference between a genital act that a married couple *renders* infertile, or an act they engage in that is not the kind of act intended by God to generate life (such as masturbation or ejaculatory oral or anal sex), and homosexual behavior. It seems many people who oppose homosexual behavior in the public square hesitate to spell out their case for fear of condemning the conduct of most heterosexuals.[9] Such is the predicament of a culture that has embraced contraception.

4. What kind of cruel God do we have that would give people these feelings and then tell them they can't act on them?

God doesn't create people with homosexual desires any more than he creates people with lust in their hearts for the opposite sex. *Both* are the result of the fallen world in which we live. In this sense, we're *all* in need of "reorienting" our sexual desires toward the truth of God's original plan.

It could be argued that lust for the opposite sex is not as drastically disordered as lust for the same sex. Even so, this shouldn't obscure the fact that we're *all* in need of healing of our sexuality. And the healing is the same for everyone: to find our true identity as men and women in Christ. I don't mean to suggest that if we just had enough faith all our problems, confusions, and wounds would disappear in a flash. It's a process, and we should make use of all that's good in psychological counseling, spiritual direction, spiritual reading, and whatever else is truly helpful on our journey (check the Resources section for suggestions in this regard).

God's call on our lives is not impossible to live. It's difficult, sometimes extremely difficult. But God never asks the impossible. That *would* be cruel. If we think our weakness is stronger than God's strength, we've emptied the cross of its power.

5. Are you saying it's possible for homosexuals to change and become heterosexual?

Before I answer the question, I need to clarify the terms being used. We use the words "homosexual" and "heterosexual" to distinguish between those who are sexually attracted to the same sex and those who are attracted to the opposite sex. They are useful words in some contexts, but there's an inherent tendency in *naming* such things that leads to treating them as concrete realities when they're not.

Evil is a useful word, for example. But evil doesn't exist in its own right. Evil is simply the absence of good, just as cold is the absence of heat, and darkness the absence of light.

My point is that "*homo*-sexuality" doesn't exist in its own right. Nor is there really any such thing as "*hetero*-sexuality." All that really exists is *sex-*

uality: the call of men and women to love in the image of God either through marriage or in celibacy. Any other desire or attraction (whether geared toward the same or opposite sex) is a privation, a lack, of this good.

Any other desire or attraction is like cold in the absence of heat, or darkness in the absence of light. Cold cannot "change" into heat. The presence of heat vanquishes cold. Darkness doesn't "change" into light. The presence of light vanquishes darkness.

Similarly, homosexuals don't "change" into heterosexuals. Men and women simply *become what they are.* That is, as the sun rises in the cold and darkness, men and women who struggle with same-sex attraction can and do experience warmth and light. The truth of sexuality can and does vanquish distortions of sexuality.

To continue with the sunrise analogy, few will ever be at "high noon" in this life with *all* the cold and darkness banished. It's probably more accurate to say we live at dawn: a mixture of light and dark, cold and warmth. But whatever our particular struggles, everyone can, through an ongoing appropriation of Christ's redemption, experience more and more the truth of sexuality as God intended it to be in the beginning. And even if not in this life, in the next life Christ will bring to completion the work he has begun in each of us (see Phil 1:6).

We must remember, however, that it's precisely *the cross* from which we receive the power to "become what we are." This means suffering. This means dying to a lifetime of diseased ways of thinking and behaving. This means letting go of the very thing, perhaps, in which a person has posited his identity, and *re-positing* that identity in the death and resurrection of Christ.

This means *it ain't easy.* I wouldn't want to imply that a person with same-sex attraction could simply rid him or herself of it just by praying hard enough or having enough faith. For those who have experienced transformation, most will attest that it comes slowly and painfully. It comes only if a person is willing to pick up his or her cross *every day.* And sometimes the cross gets heavier before it gets lighter.

So the answer to the question, with all proper clarifications, is *yes.* As numerous "former homosexuals" demonstrate, it is possible for a person even with predominant same-sex attraction, if he or she is willing and receives the proper counseling, to experience rightly ordered sexual attraction. This doesn't mean, for whatever reason, that it always happens. Nor is a person loved any less by God if he or she doesn't experience such a change.

But it *is* possible, and that should be a source of great hope for those who are seeking to overcome their struggle with same-sex attraction.[10] It should also be noted that clinical experience seems to demonstrate that to the degree a person has lived actively as a homosexual, it's more difficult to experience rightly ordered sexual desire. Conversely, those who experience the attraction but haven't acted on it usually experience transformation of their sexual desires more readily.

6. You know that a host of homosexuals would vehemently disagree with everything you're saying and accuse you of being a homophobe.

Yes, I do. But a host of others, whose voice is often silenced in the national media, would agree wholeheartedly.

In saying this, however, I'm not trying to shore up the sides of two warring camps. Even those who would vehemently disagree have something to say. Distorted as homosexual desire is, there's always an element of truth to be found in it. (A distortion, after all, is simply a twisting of truth). There's always a person behind the desire who is longing, as everyone is longing, to be loved and affirmed as a human being.

Compassion should never lead us to compromise what's true, but it *should* lead us to affirm those with same-sex attraction as human beings. It *should* lead us to reach out and listen. It *should* lead us to want to understand their struggles.

When we do reach out in love, lo and behold, those of us who think we have everything "straight" actually find that we have a lot to learn about life from the dreams and experiences, hopes and fears, of homosexuals. Charity, from both "sides," is the only human response. Dismissing those active in a "gay lifestyle" as "sinners" and "sodomites" is just as uncharitable as when they dismiss those who oppose their behavior as "homophobes."

I don't mean to ignore the fact that fear and mistreatment of homosexuals exists. More often than not, it seems this fear results in those people with a tenuous grasp on their own sexual desires. Such people often feel threatened by the mere existence of those who live active homosexual lives. They may even act violently against homosexuals in a perverse attempt to bolster their own fragile sense of gender identity, rejecting in others the confused emotions and desires that they cannot face in themselves. It shouldn't even need mentioning that such violence is unconditionally condemned by the Catholic Church.

7. I know a lesbian couple who live right across the street. They're so kind and loving toward us and toward each other. I refuse to believe that they're "living in sin."

Are you kind and loving toward your family and neighbors? Does that mean you never sin in other ways? Of course not.

Even people who base a large part of their lives on something objectively sinful are able to show genuine love and human kindness, oftentimes even more so than people who may not have anything "large and looming" on their own laundry list of sins. I'm sure you're right to say they're genuinely kind. I'm sure there are elements of genuine love that they share for one another.

Still, whatever is erotic in the love they share can only be based on a disordered understanding of themselves as women. This doesn't mean they're inherently "bad people." It just means they're in need of Christ's redemption like the rest of us.

8. I'm married with three kids. I've never admitted this to anybody, but sometimes I'm attracted to other men. Does this mean I'm gay? I'm afraid this will ruin my marriage. What should I do? How can I overcome this?

No! It does *not* mean you're gay. (Remember, no one *is* gay, ontologically speaking.) It means you live in a fallen world and are confused about your own masculine identity. Welcome to the human race.

Your struggle is *not* an insurmountable hurdle to a healthy, holy marriage. If you're committed to facing your struggles and seeking Christ's help to be the husband and father you're called to be, there should be no reason for this to ruin your relationship with your wife and kids. In fact, I've seen marriages and families grow by leaps and bounds when a spouse with same-sex attraction has sought the proper help.

How can you overcome this attraction you sometimes feel? Before offering some practical suggestions, I'll respond by telling you more about my own struggles and how the Lord has worked in my life with the hope that it may help.

As I already mentioned, as a teenager (and even into my early twenties), I went through a painful period of questioning my masculine identity. I was very troubled by the fact that I found myself somewhat attracted or drawn to men who I thought were more masculine than I. Whenever I'd be in such a person's presence (the college campus "stud," for instance), I'd feel terribly insecure about myself.

Listening to tapes of a conference on gender issues and personal healing finally helped me to make sense out of this troubling inner dynamic. Several of the talks were given by a man who had lived as an active homosexual for many years. Although I can't say my attractions were ever fully eroticized as his were, as he very candidly shared his struggles and his healings, his story resonated with me.[11]

Boys, by virtue of the fact that they're boys, have an inherent need to identify with what is masculine. They have an inherent need to *become men*. In the natural course of things a boy meets this need through healthy relationships with male role models whom he very naturally aspires to be like (such as his father, uncles, grandfathers, teachers, coaches).

In the absence of healthy relationships, that is, in the absence of male role models worth aspiring to be like, boys and young men will naturally seek to fill the void. They will admire, want to be with, and be attracted to those men whom they perceive to have "become men." This desire doesn't always become eroticized, but it can and sometimes does.[12]

The fact that most every boy hangs posters of his "heroes" on the wall points to this dynamic. Boys are looking for what it means to be a man. Unfortunately, what the world holds out is gravely distorted.

Consequently, boys and young men end up positing the meaning of manhood in all sorts of false images: the "lady's man," the "muscle man," the "*GQ* man," the "Marlboro man"—you name it. And consciously or unconsciously, they long to become the image that has lodged in their souls as the "ultimate masculine."[13] If they don't measure up to that image, they become terribly insecure, particularly in the presence of those men whom they think embody the image more than they themselves do.

This inner dynamic became a very pointed reality for me one day as I was working at one of my first jobs out of college. The woman who sat behind me was the kind of girl who hung Chippendale posters in her cubicle. These images of muscle-bound studs in tight spandex pants and bow ties tapped into all my insecurities, so I avoided her cubicle like the plague. One day I reluctantly overheard a conversation she was having with a friend. She described a dream she'd had of a similar stud who rode up the beach on his white stallion and had wild sex with her in the waves.

I'm not one prone to visions, but I had one right then and there as I was trying my darnedest not to listen to her conversation. I saw the man she described walking down the beach. He was everything that years of living in this society had convinced me it meant to be a man: muscle-bound, attractive, sleek. He wasn't just *a* man. He was *the* man. At some place in my soul, he was what *I* wanted to be, but wasn't.

Then I saw another man walking beside him. He was everything that society had convinced me was not manly. Nothing drew me to him at all. He was weak, disfigured, beaten, bloody. He wore a crown of thorns on his head and had scourge marks all over his body.

Then a voice posed a question to me. I can only assume it was the voice of God. It said: "Who is the *real* man, and with whom do you wish to identify?"

I was stunned. I realized at that moment that I had been believing, even *worshiping*, a lie.[14] I realized at that moment that all my insecurity as a man stemmed from positing my identity in a false image of masculinity.

My heart cried out: "Jesus, you're the real man. I choose to identify with you."

Then my heart sank. *Wait a minute,* I thought. *If I choose to identify with Christ, if I choose to seek the very meaning of my manhood in him, I'll be treated just like him. The world won't affirm me as a man. The world will mock me, laugh at me, spit in my face, "crucify" me.*

I shuddered. But Truth drew me to himself and gave me the grace to renounce my idol.

I've had many turning points in my life. This was certainly one of the top three. The cause of years of insecurity and fear was encapsulated for me in that vision.

Within days I purposely went into that woman's cubicle to stare those Chippendales in the face. The lie no longer had a grip on me. I was able to see those distorted images for what they were and stand secure in claiming my masculine identity in Christ.

In fact, I realized that those men should want to be like me. Not because I'm so great, but because I'm seeking Christ. I haven't been completely without my insecurities since, but there was a dramatic shift in my soul that day that continues to anchor me whenever I'm tempted to believe lies about the meaning of manhood.

There's no magic formula for healing confused emotions and desires, but based on my own experience, I offer four suggestions:

Educate yourself. Read the books I've recommended in the end notes to this chapter and any other books that present an orthodox Christian understanding of same-sex attraction.

Look into your own soul and identify the lies you believe about the meaning of manhood. Compare whatever you *think* it means to be a man with Christ. He's the true model of masculinity: *Ecce homo!* ("Behold the man!" See Jn 19:5).

To worship Christ and posit your identity in him is not idolatry because he's God! This is the image we *should* emulate because this is the image in which we're made. This is how we become what we are.

When you experience attractions to other men, learn to discern what they mean. Confused attractions most often stem from what we admire but fear we lack. When we see that particular quality in others, sometimes we want to *take it in* to ourselves so badly that it can become an obsession.

Untwist these distorted desires, and you'll find that what you desire to *take in* to yourself is Christ. And praise be to God, Christ gives us his very flesh to *eat* in the Eucharist. If you allow the Eucharist to be the wellspring of your identity as a man, you'll find you lack nothing, and confused attractions will fade.

Don't go it alone. Share your struggles with a trusted friend, spiritual director, or counselor whom you know will give you sound Christian advice. There are also group programs of healing that you may find helpful.[15]

9. Our daughter recently told us she's a lesbian and that she's moving in with her "girlfriend." It's put a terrible strain on our relationship with her. My husband and I don't know what to do or where to turn.

Certainly you already have and will continue to go through a range of emotions over your daughter's "news." Be patient with yourself as you work through your feelings, but be careful not to *act* on emotional impulse, especially in a way that would make your daughter feel isolated or ostracized. Perhaps now more than ever, your daughter needs to know that you love her. Whatever the tensions caused, don't break off contact. Don't reject her.

None of this means, however, that you must *approve* of the choices she's making with her life. In fact, it would be *unloving*, knowing what you know, *not* to challenge her—at the appropriate time, with gentleness, humility, respect, patience, and understanding—to embrace the truth of God's plan for her sexuality. Let Christ's example guide you. While he was uncompromising with sin, he was ever patient and loving toward sinners.

Perhaps the most important thing you can do for your daughter is to pray for her, not out of a sense of self-righteous indignation but out of a loving desire to see her become the woman she's created to be. Some parents in your situation fear for their child's salvation. While no one can know the state of another person's soul before God, this you can rely upon: the Lord desires her salvation more than you do yourself. Trust in his mercy. Never lose hope for your daughter's conversion of heart.

Furthermore, seek support for yourselves as parents and, if she's willing, for your daughter. *Courage* is a Church-approved support group devoted to helping Catholics who struggle with same-sex attraction to live holy, chaste lives in keeping with the Church's teachings. A sister group, called *EnCourage*, offers support to parents of children with same-sex attraction.[16]

Finally, if you're willing to receive it as such, your daughter's announcement is actually an opportunity for growth for your whole family. In our fallen world, the term "dysfunctional family" is redundant. Every family has its share of "dysfunction" because every family is made up of fallen human beings.

Certainly, no parents set out to influence a child to have homosexual feelings. So parents shouldn't blame themselves if a child does, much less take responsibility for an adult child's decisions. Still, it must be acknowledged that family dynamics often do play a role in the development of a child's problems later in life, including gender identity problems. Just as love is diffusive of itself, so are sin and dysfunctional relating.

Don't be afraid to bring the light of Christ into all the family "closets." Open wide the doors to Christ. Don't be afraid to admit and seek forgiveness from your adult children for mistakes that were made, patterns of relating that were unhealthy, and even sexual sin that may have been (or still is) part of your own marriage.

While you may think your sex life is none of your kids' business, and in some respects that's true, look at it this way: because your sex life is the very origin of your children's lives, their identity is intimately intertwined with what goes on in your bedroom. I've worked with enough wounded people to know that parental sins such as adultery, pornography, contraception, and divorce have a deep and lasting effect on children. Prudence may dictate otherwise in some situations, but open discussion with your adult children about your own failings is often a crucial step in healing family wounds. If you have reason to believe such discussions would be explosive, the presence of a wise family counselor is a good idea.

Christ entered the world through a family in order to restore the family. He can bring healing and forgiveness. Let him.

Nine

Saying "I Do" to God Alone

Sex and the Celibate Vocation

Then I saw a new heaven and a new earth; for the first heaven and the first earth had passed away, and the sea was no more. And I saw the holy city, new Jerusalem, coming down out of heaven from God, prepared as a bride adorned for her husband; and I heard a great voice from the throne saying, "Behold, the dwelling of God is with men."

St. John the Apostle[1]

Sex and the celibate vocation? Isn't that a contradiction of terms? More aptly, it's a *paradox*.

We can't understand the Christian mystery without facing the tension of paradox. We must affirm the truth of one God in three Persons; of the Man who is also God; of the Virgin who is also Mother. In marriage, two become one flesh. In our walk with God, we must die to live, surrender to be free, lose our life to find it.

These are not the teachings of a schizophrenic God or a Church gone mad. If they strike us as "double-speak," it's because we don't yet think with the mind of God.

Marriage, sex, and the celibate vocation are much more interrelated than we might first think. They're also interdependent. When each is given proper esteem and respect, the delicate balance among them is maintained.

On the other hand, if any of the three (marriage, sex, or celibacy) is devalued, overvalued, or otherwise disrespected, the others inevitably suffer. It's no coincidence, for example, that the sexual revolution brought both a dramatic rise in divorce *and* a dramatic decline in vocations to the priesthood and religious life. Nor is it any coincidence that historical misinterpretations of the celibate vocation have led to a disparagement of sex and marriage.

All such error stems from failure to deal with the tension of paradox. There's something mentally torturous about reconciling the (seemingly) irreconcilable poles of paradox. So to avoid the discomfort we focus on one aspect of a truth and end up denying others.

But it's precisely by *pressing into* the tension of paradox that we discover the fullness of truth. We must find our home in that tension. Only then can we properly understand the profound interrelationship among marriage, sex, and the celibate vocation.

1. If the call to "nuptial love" is the fundamental truth of our existence and the way we fulfill ourselves as human beings, why does the Church promote celibacy?

At first glance it seems as if the Church's promotion of celibacy is a contradiction of everything we've said about the dignity and importance of sex and marriage. Upon further investigation, however, we discover that the celibate vocation is actually the ultimate *fulfillment* of everything we've discussed.

As a sacrament, the "one flesh" union of marriage is only a sign and foreshadowing of things to come. We're created for nuptial union with God. That's what sexual desire ultimately points us to—our desire for heaven.

There, Christ will make a gift of himself to humanity in a beatifying experience completely beyond anything proper to earthly life. Our reciprocal gift of self will be our response to the gift of the Bridegroom.[2] The marriage of divinity and humanity will be eternally consummated. (See chapter three, question 17.)

Only by looking toward this heavenly reality can we properly understand the celibate vocation. As we read in the gospel, Christ calls some of his followers to embrace celibacy, not for celibacy's sake but "for the sake of the kingdom" (Mt 19:12). "The kingdom" is precisely *the heavenly marriage*. In short, those who choose celibacy are "skipping" the sacrament in anticipation of the real thing. By expressing the "I do" of a marriage commitment directly to God, celibates step beyond the dimension of history—while living within the dimension of history—and dramatically declare to the world that the kingdom of God is here (see Mt 12:28).

Both vocations, then, in their own particular way, are a fulfillment of the call to "nuptial love" revealed through our bodies. As John Paul II says: "On the basis of the same nuptial meaning of being as a body, male or female, there can be formed the love that commits Man to marriage for the whole duration of his life, but there can be formed also the love that commits Man to a life of continence for the sake of the kingdom of heaven."[3]

We can't escape the call of our sexuality. Every man, by virtue of the fact that he's a man, is called to be both a husband and a father; and every woman, by virtue of the fact that she's a woman, is called to be both a wife and a mother—either through marriage or through the celibate vocation. Celibate men become an "icon" of Christ; their bride is the Church. Celibate women become an "icon" of the Church; their bridegroom is Christ. And both bear many spiritual children.

Thus the terms father, mother, brother, and sister are applicable to marriage *and* celibacy. Both vocations are indispensable in building the family of God. Each vocation complements the other and demonstrates the other's meaning. Marriage reveals the nuptial character of celibacy, and celibacy reveals that the ultimate purpose of marriage is to prepare us for heaven.

2. Does the Church still teach that celibacy is a "higher" calling than marriage?

Yes, but this must be carefully qualified. History has seen some grave distortions of St. Paul's teaching that he who marries does "well," but he who refrains does "better" (see 1 Cor 7:38). It's led some to view marriage as a second-class vocation for those who can't handle celibacy. It's also solidified people's erroneous suspicions that sex is inherently tainted, and that only those who abstain can be truly "holy." Such errors have led John Paul II to assert firmly: "The 'superiority' of continence to matrimony in the authentic Tradition of the Church never means disparagement of marriage or belittlement of its essential value. It does not mean any shift whatsoever in a Manichean direction."[4]

Celibacy is "better" or "higher" than marriage in the sense that heaven is better or higher than earth. Remember that celibacy is not a *sacrament* of heaven on earth. It *is* in some sense heaven on earth. But this shouldn't lead those who are called to marriage to devalue their vocation.

Everyone is called to a life of holiness by responding to the call to "nuptial love" stamped in his or her body. But not everyone is called in the same way: "Each has his own special gift from God, one of one kind and one of another" (1 Cor 7:7).

Each of us should respond to the gift we've been given. If we're called to celibacy, then we shouldn't choose marriage. If we're called to marriage, then we shouldn't choose celibacy. Hence the important need to discern our vocation prayerfully.

3. Why aren't Catholic priests allowed to be married?

Actually, some Catholic priests *are* allowed to be married. We often forget in the West that there are many Eastern rite Catholic Churches (that is, Churches of the East in full communion with the pope) that have married priests. They are no less Catholic priests than priests of the Roman rite, which maintains a celibate priesthood. Furthermore, in some cases, married priests from other denominations (Anglican, for example) who convert to the Catholic faith are able to be ordained as married priests in the Roman rite.

Thus celibacy isn't essential to a valid priesthood. It's simply a discipline upheld in the Western Church in order to conform more closely to the example of Christ.

Christ was not married to one particular woman because he came to marry *the whole human race*. The Church is his eternal Bride. Ordained priests become a sacrament of Christ. They make the love of the heavenly Bridegroom efficaciously present to the Church, particularly in the Eucharistic sacrifice. Acting in the person of Christ, priests also marry the Church.

This important symbolism is better retained when a priest is not also married to a particular woman. As St. Paul said, the celibate is not "divided" in his service, but is able to devote himself entirely to the service of the Church (see 1 Cor 7:32-34).

I think it's unfortunate in some ways that we define celibacy with a word that points to what it has given up rather than defining it in terms of what it has *embraced*. Much confusion could be avoided if we described the celibate vocation as the "heavenly marriage," for instance. This is the marriage in which priests and all consecrated celibate persons participate.

4. Celibacy is simply unnatural. It's no wonder that so many priests have sexual problems. This type of scandal would end if priests were allowed to marry.

In some sense you're right to say celibacy is *un*-natural. As Christ reveals, celibacy is *super*-natural. It's celibacy for the sake of the kingdom. By calling some to renounce the natural call to marriage, Christ established an entirely new way of life, and in doing so, he demonstrated the power of the cross to transform lives.

For those who are stuck in a fallen view of sex with no concept of the freedom to which we're called in Christ, the idea of lifelong celibacy is complete nonsense. But for those who have experienced the transformation of their sexual desires in Christ, the idea of making a complete gift of our sexuality to God not only becomes a possibility; it becomes very attractive. The celibate vocation is *not* a rejection of sexuality. If some approach it this way, according to John Paul II, they're not living in accord with Christ's words.[5]

Celibacy is a grace, a gift. Only a small minority of Christ's followers are given this gift. But those who *are* given this gift are also given the grace to be faithful to their vows, just as married couples are given the grace to be faithful to their vows.

In both vocations people can and do reject this grace and violate their vows. Certainly there's a need in the typical Catholic diocese for greater openness about sexual woundedness and for development and promotion of ministries that bring Christ's healing to those in need, including priests. But the solution to marital and celibate infidelity is not to concede to human weakness and redefine the nature of the commitments. The solution is to point to the cross as the font of grace that it is, a font from which we can drink freely and receive *real power* to live and love as we're called.

Furthermore, the statistical rates of sexual misconduct among celibate priests is no higher than that of clergy in Christian denominations who are allowed to marry. There is absolutely no evidence that allowing priests to marry would solve or even alleviate this problem.

There's also a dangerously misguided approach to marriage inherent in the idea that marriage is the solution to the sexual scandal of priests. As has been stressed throughout this book, marriage does not provide a "legitimate outlet" for disordered sexual desire. Celibacy does not *cause* sexual disorder. Sin does. Simply getting married does not *cure* sexual disorder. Christ does. If a priest, or any other man, were to enter marriage with deep-seated sexual disorders, he would be condemning his wife to a life of sexual objectification. The only way the scandal of sexual sin (whether committed by priests or others) will end is if people experience the redemption of their sexuality in Christ.

5. Why can't women be priests?

For many women, the fact that the Catholic Church reserves priestly ordination to men stirs a caldron of intense emotion fired by the "historical consciousness" of women's oppression. Only in recent years, it seems, has the Church been willing to acknowledge and ask forgiveness for the fact that, as John Paul II expressed in his *Letter to Women*, "objective blame [for this oppression], especially in particular historical contexts, has belonged to not just a few members of the Church. May this regret," he continues, "be transformed, on the part of the whole Church, into a renewed commitment of fidelity to the Gospel vision."[6]

This gospel vision is precisely what we've been discussing throughout this book: the great "nuptial mystery" of Christ's union with the Church symbolized from the beginning by our creation as male and female. Fidelity to this vision calls us to uphold woman's dignity at every turn and to resist the ways in which gender roles have been exaggerated to favor men. But it also calls us to resist the other extreme that views men and women as interchangeable.

As mentioned previously, equality between the sexes doesn't mean *sameness*. It's the fundamental *difference* of the sexes that reveals the great "nuptial mystery." It's the fundamental *difference* of the sexes that quite literally brings life to the world.

A culture that levels this difference is a culture committing suicide, a culture of death. Professor Stanislaw Grygiel, vice-president of the John Paul II Institute for Studies on Marriage and Family, aptly described the danger of a "unisex" world in the quote that begins the previous chapter. As a preface to that statement, he said that to understand "the miracle of sexual difference ... is the beginning of a path in which we discover the ultimate and fundamental difference for human beings: the difference between God and [humanity].'"[7] To blur sexual difference is to blur the great nuptial mystery: the call to life-giving communion between man and woman, and between God and humanity.

Men and women have different callings in this life-giving communion. It's the bridegroom who gives the seed, and the bride who conceives life within her. One role isn't better than the other. Both are equally dignified and indispensable.

We must receive the calling we've been given as a gift from God if we are ever to be at peace with ourselves. Should men complain that God hasn't given them the privilege of being mothers? For a woman to want to be an ordained priest is similarly misguided.

We call priests *father* for a reason. Priests efficaciously symbolize Christ's giving up his body for his Bride so that she can conceive life "in the Holy Spirit." Only men can do this. As John Paul II reminds us: "It is *the Eucharist that above all expresses the redemptive act of Christ the Bridegroom towards the Church, the Bride.* This is clear and unambiguous when the sacramental ministry of the Eucharist, in which the priest acts 'in the person of Christ,' is performed by a man."[8]

If the ministry of the Eucharist were performed by a woman, the symbolism would become that of bride to bride. There would be no possibility of effecting nuptial union, and thus no possibility of new life coming to the Church. Here we see again how intimately united the marital embrace is with the Eucharist. John Paul II sums it up this way: *"The Eucharist is ... the sacrament of the Bridegroom and of the Bride."*[9]

6. If even men become the "bride of Christ" as members of the Church, why can't women become the bridegroom as a priest?

First, a brief discussion of the masculine and feminine principles in each of us. If it's male and female *together* that encompasses what's human, and if every man and woman is not merely half human but *fully* human, then it's proper to conclude that every man and woman is an interior "marriage" of masculinity and femininity. Thus in some sense we can speak of feminine principles in men and masculine principles in women.

Still, this interior marriage manifests itself as essentially *male* in men and *female* in women. The Church, in turn, as a "corporate person," is a marriage of men and women that manifests itself essentially as *feminine*, as *Bride*. There are masculine and feminine principles in this Bride in which both men and women partake. As much as men become "bride" as members of the Church, women become "priest" as members of the priesthood of all believers (see 1 Pt 2:9). Every baptized man *and woman* participates in Christ's priesthood by living a sacrificial life in union with him.

But we enter a different realm as soon as we talk about an individual person becoming a *sacrament* of Christ. For sacraments to be efficacious, the physical reality must properly symbolize the spiritual reality. For instance, if a priest said the words of baptism over someone while pouring motor oil over his head, there would be no sacrament because the cleansing symbolism of water is necessary to bring about the spiritual cleansing from sin. Without an accurate symbol (motor oil symbolizes making dirty), nothing happens.[10]

Similarly, if a bishop laid hands on a woman and proclaimed the words of ordination, nothing would happen because a woman is not an accurate symbol of the Bridegroom. So it's not a matter of the Church's stubborn unwillingness to ordain women to the priesthood. It's a matter of *impossibility*.

7. Didn't St. Paul say there is no longer male or female, but all are one in Christ Jesus?

Yes (see Gal 3:28). But how do we become *one* in Christ Jesus? Specifically through the *difference* of the sexes. Sexual union symbolizes union in Christ. Husband and wife are no longer two (male and female) but one. Yet the only way they can become one is by being *male* and *female* first. Thus St. Paul is not leveling sexual difference but showing where it leads—to unity in Christ.

8. I'm single. If "nuptial love" is so important, what about me?

There's a difference, I'd say, between a person who chooses to remain single in the world in order to devote him or herself to worthy causes and a person who is single not by choice but by circumstance. The former has made a vocational choice in some ways parallel to the celibate vocation and, by living a life in service to others, is fulfilling the call to make a sincere gift of self in imitation of Christ. The latter is, in some sense, still waiting to make that definitive gift of self.

This doesn't mean that the latter person's life need remain on hold. He or she can live a very fruitful life as a gift to others while maintaining the hope of one day finding a spouse and making a definitive vocational choice.

In any case, no one should think his or her life is meaningless without a spouse. The ultimate meaning of life is *heavenly marriage*. This is the gift Christ offers *everyone*—the gift of his very self.

Accepting this gift and giving ourselves back to Christ is how we *all* fulfill our call to nuptial love, whether we're married or not. In fact, if we're seeking our ultimate fulfillment in earthly marriage, we're setting ourselves up for serious disillusionment. As the saying goes, never hang your hat on a hook that can't bear the weight.

9. Why didn't Joseph and Mary have sex if they were married?

Ah! A great question with which to conclude this chapter and this book. In fact, in some ways Joseph and Mary's marriage provides a summary of everything I've tried to say.

Joseph and Mary's marriage is a paradox within a paradox, a "double mystery," so to speak. Marriage is itself a mysterious paradox in that the *two* become *one* through sexual union. But the marriage of Joseph and Mary is doubly mysterious and paradoxical because *they never had sexual union*. What could this possibly mean? To the extent that we can know it, the great "nuptial mystery" of the universe is actually revealed through this virginal marriage.

God gave Joseph and Mary an exceptional calling: to live the marital vocation *and* the celibate vocation *at the same time*. Remember what the celibate vocation is? It's the heavenly marriage. Joseph and Mary's marriage is the union of earthly marriage and heavenly marriage. *It's the marriage of heaven and earth.*

And what's the fruit of this celibate marriage? *The Word made flesh.* The fruit of their heavenly and earthly marriage is the wedding of the divine and human in one flesh—Jesus Christ, the center of the universe and of history.[11]

This is why the Church's teaching on sex is good news. From the beginning, the "one flesh" union of Adam and Eve was a foreshadowing of the Incarnation. God created sex as the fundamental revelation in creation of his plan of life and love—his plan to share his eternal life and love with us by becoming one in the flesh with us.

This is the great "nuptial mystery" of the universe in which we're all called to participate. This is why we crave sexual union: because we crave union with God. This is why the devil so often tempts us to distort sexual union: because he wants to keep us from union with God.

Don't fall for his lies. Live according to the truth of your sexuality, and you'll fulfill the very meaning of your being and existence. Live according to the truth of your sexuality, and you'll one day live forever in the eternal climax of the nuptial union of Christ and the Church.

I pray this book has been of service to you in your journey toward this eternal embrace.

Come, Lord. Let it be done to us, your Bride, as you will. Amen.

Notes

Introduction

1. *Redemptor Hominis*, n. 10.

2. The *Theology of the Body* is the collective title given to the 129 homilies John Paul II delivered in his Wednesday General Audiences between September 5, 1979, and November 28, 1984. In them, through a searching analysis of biblical texts that speak of the body, sex, marriage, and the celibate vocation, John Paul presents a depth of understanding of the human person and the meaning of our call to "nuptial love" never before articulated. Many of these insights are set forth in chapter one of this book. Subsequent chapters also draw heavily from this work. Hereafter, we will refer to it simply as *Body*, followed by the date of the General Audience cited.

   The entire catechesis was originally published by the Daughters of St. Paul in four volumes now out of print (*Original Unity of Man and Woman, Blessed Are the Pure of Heart, The Theology of Marriage and Celibacy,* and *Reflections on Humanae Vitae*). Quotes used in this book are taken from this translation. A slightly different translation of the theology of the body has more recently been published in one volume, also by the Daughters of St. Paul. To order it, see the Resources section at the back of this book, which includes that ministry's phone number. Also listed there is information on a tape series entitled *Naked Without Shame*, which seeks to make the revolutionary insights of John Paul's *Theology of the Body* accessible to a larger audience.

3. This work was written in 1981 following the 1980 Synod of Bishops on the Family. It's an excellent and comprehensive presentation of Catholic teaching on sex, marriage, and family life. Hereafter, in the notes we will refer to it as *Familiaris*.

4. Karol Wojtyla (John Paul II), *Love and Responsibility* (San Francisco: Ignatius, 1993), 43 (hereafter referred to as *Love*). This work was first published in Poland in 1960, eighteen years before Karol Wojtyla was to become Pope John Paul II. Based on years of dialogue and pastoral work with young men and women, as well as engaged and married couples, the book examines ordinary human experience to demonstrate that Catholic moral teaching on sex and marriage corresponds perfectly with the dignity of the human person.

   A "personalist" philosophy, as John Paul's position has been called, recognizes that persons are subjects toward whom the only proper attitude is love. A person must never be made merely an object of use. He argues that failure to accept the demands of the Catholic sexual ethic inevitably turns people into objects to be used.

ONE

The Great Mystery

1. John Paul II, *Letter to Families*, n. 19 (hereafter referred to as *Families*).
2. See *Body*, January 16, 1980.
3. *Body*, January 16, 1980.
4. See *Families*, n. 19.
5. We must be careful not to misunderstand what's being said. The fact that our sexuality reveals something of the mystery of the Trinity does not mean that the Trinity is sexual. God is not made in humanity's image as male and female, but humanity in God's. See the *Catechism of the Catholic Church*, n. 370 (hereafter referred to as *Catechism*).
6. See *Body*, January 5, 1983. John Paul II brings a development to the Church's understanding of the sacramental sign of marriage. Historically, most theologians posited the sign of marriage in the exchange of wedding vows, as opposed to another view that posited the sacramental sign in the act of consummation. John Paul II brings the two views together by recognizing that the words of the wedding vows "can be fulfilled only by conjugal intercourse." In conjugal intercourse, he says, "we pass to the reality which corresponds to these words. Both the one and the other element are important in regard to the structure of the sacramental sign."
7. Someone might object: "Hasn't science disproved all that Adam and Eve stuff?" No. The creation stories in Genesis were never intended to be a *scientific* account of how the world was created. Genesis uses figurative language that speaks of much deeper truths about the universe, and our existence in it, than science can ever tell us.

   Suppose you asked a scientist and a poet both to describe a tree. They would give very different reports. Could one say that the scientist disproves the poet?

   Still, the creation stories in Genesis are not merely someone's poetry. While they're mythical, they're not just a myth. They are the inspired Word of God. They speak truth—deep truth—about the meaning of life, who God is, and who we are as men and women. The Church interprets the symbolism of biblical language in an authentic way, teaching that our first parents were constituted in a state of holiness and justice but fell through a deed that took place at the beginning of human history (see *Catechism*, nn. 375 and 390).
8. At this point in the story, "Adam" (which literally means "man") is a generic human person and represents all humanity, not just the male. In fact, the biblical account does not make the distinction between male and female until the woman is created from Adam's side.
9. *Gaudium et Spes*, n. 24 (hereafter referred to as *Gaudium*). Being created for "our own sake" means, among other things, that we can never rightly be *used* as a means to another person's end. In contrast, the rest of creation is created not for "its own sake" but for *our* sake. So long as we are good stewards, we can *use* the created world for our benefit. But we must never *use* another person.

10. See *Body*, November 7, 1979, note 15. (This is note 4 in *Original Unity of Man and Woman*.)

11. *Body*, January 16, 1980.

12. *Catechism*, n. 391.

13. See *Body*, October 31, 1979.

14. This is a generalization, of course. But it does seem to be true for the most part that men experience their fallen sexual desires as geared toward physical gratification at the expense of a woman, while women experience their fallen sexual desires as geared toward emotional gratification at the expense of a man. It should also be mentioned here that some men and women experience sexual desires toward members of the same sex. While same-sex attractions, since they are most often not freely chosen, are not in themselves sinful, they are, to be sure, part of the disorder of the sexual appetite caused by original sin. See chapter eight for more discussion of this matter.

15. *Body*, October 8, 1980.

16. See *Body*, March 5, 1980.

17. See *Catechism*, n. 411.

18. It's important to realize that the marriage of the New Adam and Eve is a "mystical" marriage. It takes place beyond the realm of blood and family relationships as we understand them. "Adam-Christ" and "Eve-Mary" are to be understood as archetypes of "man" and "woman." There is no reason, then, to be troubled by the fact that it is Christ's mother according to flesh and blood who, in some sense, represents all of us as Christ's mystical Bride (see *Catechism*, n. 773). Furthermore, when Jesus wants us to understand Mary as the New Eve, both at Cana and at Calvary, he doesn't refer to her as his mother but as "the woman"—a reference to Genesis 3:15.

19. As John Paul II says, "All human beings—both women and men—are called through the Church, to be the 'Bride' of Christ.... In this way 'being the bride,' and thus the 'feminine' element, becomes a symbol of all that is 'human'"(*Mulieris Dignitatem*, n. 25). Elsewhere in the same text he says, "From this point of view, woman is the representative and the archetype of the whole human race: she represents the humanity which belongs to all human beings, both men and women" (n. 4).

20. *Catechism*, n. 1617.

21. St. Paul speaks beautifully of how the cross sets us free from sin and how the Holy Spirit empowers us to love in Romans chapters 6, 7, and 8. Also see Galatians chapter 5.

TWO
Who Says?

1. See *Catechism*, n. 889.

2. *Lumen Gentium*, n. 12.

3. See *Catechism*, n. 889.
4. This has only happened twice in the history of the Church. In 1854 Pope Pius IX infallibly defined the dogma of the Immaculate Conception (the teaching that, in light of Christ's redemptive work, Mary was conceived without original sin). And in 1950 Pope Pius XII infallibly defined the dogma of Mary's Assumption, body and soul, into heaven.
5. See *Lumen Gentium*, n. 25.
6. *Catechism*, n. 2051, emphasis added.
7. *Catechism*, n. 892.
8. For an excellent study of the essential role of hierarchy in the ordering of not only the Church but society at large, see Joyce Little's, *The Church and the Culture War* (San Francisco: Ignatius, 1995). Some of the thoughts expressed here were gleaned from her insightful work.
9. *Familiaris*, n. 9.
10. Whatever your questions, you'll always do best by going to the source for answers, such as the *Catechism*. This is the sure norm for knowing what the Church teaches and believes. Books like the one you're now reading, that attempt to explain what the Church really teaches and why, are also a great resource. Furthermore, there are various apostolates within the Church whose purpose is to clarify and explain the official teachings of the Catholic faith. Two such organizations are *Catholic Answers* and *Catholics United for the Faith*. Both organizations can answer your questions over the phone and have innumerable books, pamphlets, tapes, and other resources that explain what the Church really teaches and why. (See Resources section.)
11. To demonstrate this ambivalence, consider how many slang terms you know for your elbow. In contrast, how many slang terms do you know for those parts of the body that distinguish men and women from each other? Makes you wonder, doesn't it?
12. Credit is due to Christopher Derrick and his book *Sex and Sacredness* (San Francisco: Ignatius, 1982) for many of the insights expressed here.
13. See *Body*, October 13, 1982.
14. *Body*, October 13, 1982, n. 11.
15. See *Body*, October 29, 1980.
16. See *Body*, October 8, 1980.

THREE
What Are You Saying "I Do" To?

1. John Paul II, "The Love Within Families," *Origins* 16 (April 23, 1987): 799.
2. See *Gaudium*, n. 48, and *Code of Canon Law*, Canon 1055.
3. See *Gaudium*, n. 49.

4. Even if a marriage is not consummated, no human power can claim to dissolve it. However, the Church, in very rare cases, does have the more than human power, given by God, to dissolve nonconsummated marriages.
5. *Gaudium*, n. 48.
6. See Canon 1055.
7. *Familiaris*, n. 13
8. *Baltimore Catechism*, n. 304.
9. See Tertullian, *On the Resurrection of the Flesh*, chapter 8.
10. *Body*, February 20, 1980.
11. See *Body*, October 13, 1982.
12. *Body*, October 20, 1982.
13. *Body*, September 29, 1982.
14. In Catholic Churches of the Eastern rite, however, the priest is understood as the minister of the sacrament of marriage (see *Catechism*, n. 1623).
15. I'd recommend *Annulment, the Wedding That Was* by Rev. Michael Smith Foster (New York: Paulist, 1999). Written in question-and-answer format, it makes complex issues of canon law easy to understand. It can be ordered through the Daughters of St. Paul (see the Resources section).
16. Canons 1083–1090.
17. Men who are already married may be ordained as permanent deacons. If a deacon's wife dies, however, he is not free to remarry.
18. Canon 1108.
19. Canons 1095, 1102, 1103.
20. *Familiaris*, n. 32.
21. *Body*, September 1, 1982.

FOUR

What to Do Before "I Do"

1. John Paul II, "The Love Within Families," 799.
2. *Love*, 139.
3. See *Body*, January 26, 1983.
4. Sounds serious. It is. Seems like very few people understand this. You're right. Our culture continually bombards us with a very different message about sex. And Catholics and other Christians have not been immune to the message.

   A survey I conducted in the archdiocese of Denver indicates that 91 percent of couples involved in Catholic marriage preparation are sexually active before marriage. But the same survey also indicates that this stems more from ignorance of the Church's vision of sex than from steadfast opposition to it. When the Church's vision is presented and explained, the majority of people respond positively to it.

   It's not a message of condemnation. It's a call to live a new life in Christ. It's inviting. It's attractive. It's what every human heart desires, because it's the truth for which every human heart longs.

5. George Weigel, *Witness to Hope* (New York: Harper Collins, 1999), 343.

6. Larry Bumpass and James Sweet, *Cohabitation, Marriage, and Union Stability: Preliminary Findings* (Madison: Center for Demography and Ecology, University of Wisconsin, 1995), Working Paper #65; Alfred DeMaris and Vaninadha Rao, "Premarital Cohabitation and Subsequent Marital Stability in the United States: A Reassessment," *Journal of Marriage & the Family* 54 (1992): 179–90.

7. J.D. Teachman, J. Thomas, and K. Paasch, "Legal Status and the Stability of Coresidential Unions," *Demography* (November 1991): 571–83.

8. Premarital sex almost always involves the consistent use of contraception. Yet even if a couple engaging in premarital sex were desirous of conceiving a child, they could not be considered "open to life" in the full sense of that expression. A proper openness to life is inherently marital—that is, it recognizes the right of the child to be conceived by parents who are already committed by marriage to the child's upbringing in a stable, loving environment.

9. See "Sexual Exclusivity Among Dating, Cohabiting, and Married Women," *Journal of Marriage and the Family* 58 (1996): 33–47.

10. Even if a person is willing to or *wants* to be used, we are *never* to use. Our dignity is not contingent upon our awareness of it. In fact, if a person is unaware of his or her dignity, we are all the more obliged to show that person his or her dignity through our love.

11. See *Love*, 43.

12. *Catechism*, n. 2350.

13. Paul Quay, *The Christian Meaning of Human Sexuality* (San Francisco: Ignatius, 1985), 74–75.

14. See *Catechism*, n. 2352.

15. The disordering of the passions caused by original sin is called *concupiscence*. Concupiscence, in its broader sense, encompasses more than the disordering of the sexual appetite. Concupiscence inclines us toward sin but isn't sinful in itself, because it's not freely chosen. It's simply a "given" of fallen human nature.

16. *Love*, 46.

17. *Body*, November 12, 1980.

18. There is, however, somewhat of a female counterpart to pornography—"steamy" romance novels. The fact that women are much more drawn to these than to pornography speaks very pointedly of the female psyche. Pictures alone don't cut it for most women. They need the story, the enchanting romance, the build-up of emotion and drama.

Despite the fact that such novels are more socially acceptable than pornography, they are no less a distortion of man and woman's relationship. Both are appealing to the fallen impulse in us for sexual gratification, just in different ways. Pornography indulges the fallen male desire for physical and visual stimulation, while steamy romance novels indulge the fallen female desire for emotional and romantic stimulation. Neither one is healthy. Neither one forms us in the truth. In fact, they both form us in a lie.

19. See *Body*, October 29, 1980.
20. *Body*, December 3, 1980.
21. Since most men in our culture have been so conditioned by pornography, and by the media image of women in general, women are put under a tremendous burden to measure up in order to be found attractive. Most of these portrayals of women aren't even real. They're altered by computers to remove every trace of "blemishes" (in essence, every trace of normal humanity).

    So women are left trying to reach a standard of "beauty" that is quite literally impossible to reach. The rise in various eating disorders among women and even young girls is one pointed example of the effects that a pornographic media culture has on the female psyche. Plain and simple, pornography degrades women terribly.

    The band Tears for Fears once wrote a song called "Woman in Chains" that captures remarkably well the way men's lusts affect women. If you can find a copy, it's well worth pondering the lyrics: "Deep in your heart there are wounds time can't heal, ... it's a world gone crazy, keeps woman in chains."
22. See *Body*, March 18, 1981.
23. One place you might start in looking for help is the Christian Alliance for Sexual Recovery. See the Resources section for contact information.

FIVE
"I Do"-ing It

1. *Body*, November 21, 1984.
2. *Love*, 225.
3. See *Love*, 233.
4. *Love*, 234.
5. See John Harvey, "Expressing Marital Love During the Fertile Phase," *International Review of Natural Family Planning* (Winter 1981): 207.
6. See Canon 1061.
7. Quay, 83.
8. In *Love and Responsibility* (see pp. 270–78), John Paul II makes a distinction between "technique" in marital relations and the "culture of marital relations." The very term "technique" implies an artificial or depersonalizing analysis of sexual intimacy. A proper "culture of marital relations," on the other hand, leads to true fulfillment because it allows both husband and wife to penetrate and experience each other's "worlds." Disinterested (altruistic) tenderness in marital relations, he says, affords "the ability to enter readily into the other's emotions and experiences [which] can play a big part in the harmonization of marital intercourse."

For example, on the husband's part, this disinterested tenderness leads him to understand his wife's more gradual rise in sexual arousal and to control his own response so as to bring his wife to climax with him. Without such tenderness, there is the danger that the husband may seek just to subject his wife to the demands of his own body. So with motives always of love, spouses deliberately work at their timing in order to bring each other to the fullness of joy in their union. This is quite a different thing from the hedonistic attempt to maximize physical pleasure.

9. *Body*, June 27, 1984.
10. Talking through your experiences with a spiritual director or counselor is very helpful. There are also various programs (some better than others) designed specifically to help adults deal with sexual and relational wounds from the past in order to build healthy relationships in the present and future. One such program is called Living Waters; for contact information, see the Resources section.

    If you've been abused sexually, I would strongly urge you to seek professional counseling. For counseling over the phone, or for a referral in your area, call the Counseling Hotline of Gregory Popcak (see the Resources section).
11. *Body*, July 30, 1980.
12. The language of the Church has changed since the Second Vatican Council in defining the ends of marriage. The *Catechism* now speaks of the "twofold end" of marriage as the "good of the spouses themselves and the transmission of life" (n. 2363). This change in language stems in part from a development in understanding of the role of conjugal love in the relationship of the spouses.

    Those who sought to find the place of conjugal love within the traditional hierarchy of ends too often equated it with the *mutual help of the spouses*. This secondary end of marriage actually refers to the help and support that sharing a common life as husband and wife affords on a very practical level. Equating *mutual help* with "mutual love" led to the mistake that the Church taught that procreation takes precedence over love.

    The Second Vatican Council clarified the matter beautifully by demonstrating that conjugal love is not an *end* of marriage at all. It's the very *essence* of the marital relationship from which the ends of marriage flow. The ends of marriage are one and the same as the ends of conjugal love.

    As Vatican II stated, "By their very nature, the institution of matrimony itself *and conjugal love* are ordained for the procreation and education of children" (*Gaudium*, n. 48, emphasis added). "In this renewed formulation," says John Paul II, "the traditional teaching on the purposes of marriage (and their hierarchy) is reaffirmed and at the same time deepened from the viewpoint of the interior life of the spouses ..." (*Body*, October 10, 1984).
13. See *Body*, November 7, 1984.
14. See *Body*, July 7, 1982.

SIX

"I Do ... Not"

1. Deuteronomy 30:19.
2. Ronald Lawler, Joseph Boyle, and William May, *Catholic Sexual Ethics* (Huntington, Ind.: Our Sunday Visitor, 1985 and 1998).
3. See *Familiaris*, n. 32.
4. Ninety-nine percent effectiveness means that out of one hundred couples following the rules of NFP for one year, only one couple would conceive a child.

    See the booklet *The Effectiveness of Natural Family Planning* for the results of several different studies that confirm this figure (Cincinnati, Ohio: Couple to Couple League, 1986). To order, see contact information for the Couple to Couple League in the Resources section.
5. *L'Osservatore Romano*, October 10, 1983, 7.
6. *Humanae Vitae*, n. 16; emphasis added.
7. God also gave us the intelligence to create atomic bombs. This doesn't mean it's intelligent to do so.
8. Listen to the audiotape "Contraception, Why Not?" To order from One More Soul, see contact information in the Resources section.
9. I'm indebted to Dr. Donald DeMarco for this analogy. See his book *New Perspectives on Contraception* (Dayton, Ohio: One More Soul, 1999), 114. To order, see contact information for One More Soul in the Resources section.
10. Traditional interpretations of this passage have always seen in it God's condemnation of any and every method of deliberately sterile orgasm (masturbation, contraception, sodomy, etc.). The term "Onanism" was coined specifically in reference to such behaviors. Only modern proponents of contraception, it seems, have sought to avoid the conclusion that God slew Onan for spilling his seed.
11. This anti-child mentality is epitomized in a catalog I once saw selling a doormat that read: "Pets welcome. Children must be on a leash." The caption below the picture proclaimed, "This unwelcome mat is guaranteed to keep Fertile Myrtle and her rambunctious brood at bay."
12. *Gaudium*, n. 50.
13. *Catechism*, n. 2368.
14. *Familiaris*, n. 86.
15. Unless otherwise noted, the following statements were cited in Patrick Fagan, "A Culture of Inverted Sexuality," *Catholic World Report*, November 1998, 57. (Credit is also due Patrick Fagan for some of the thoughts presented in response to question 14.)
16. T.S. Eliot, *Thoughts after Lambeth* (London: Faber and Faber, 1931), 32.
17. "Forgetting Religion," *The Washington Post*, March 22, 1931.
18. See the following studies:

    Larry L. Bumpass and James A. Sweet, "Cohabitation, Marriage, and Union

Stability: Preliminary Findings," *NSFH Working Paper n. 65.* (Madison, Wis.: Center for Demography and Ecology: University of Wisconsin-Madison), 1995.

Maggie Gallagher, "Fatherless Boys Grow Up Into Dangerous Men," *The Wall Street Journal,* December 1, 1998, A22.

Sara McLanahan and Gary Sandefur, "The Consequences of Single Motherhood," *The American Prospect* 18 (1994): 48–58.

David Blankenhorn, *Fatherless America: Confronting Our Most Urgent Social Problem* (New York: Basic Books, 1995).

19. Philip F. Lawler, "The Price of Virtue," *Catholic World Report,* July 1997, 58.

20. Allan C. Carlson, "The Ironic Protestant Reversal: How the Original Family Movement Swallowed the Pill," *Family Policy* 12 (1999): 20.

21. For a wealth of interesting information on what early feminists thought of contraception see Linda Gordon, "Voluntary Motherhood: The Beginning of Feminist Birth Control Ideas in the United States," *Feminist Studies* 1 (Winter-Spring 1973): 5–22.

22. This shift in the feminist approach to contraception is due largely to the influence of Margaret Sanger and Planned Parenthood, the institution she founded. For a shocking look into the influence of Planned Parenthood on the modern world's view of human life and sexual morality, see Robert Marshal and Charles Donovan, *Blessed Are the Barren: The Social Policy of Planned Parenthood* (San Francisco: Ignatius, 1991).

23. Quoted from Donald Demarco's article "Contraception and the Trivialization of Sex," retrieved from www.cuf.org/july99a.htm, 6.

24. *Humanae Vitae,* n. 17.

25. John Paul II, *Evangelium Vitae,* n. 13.

26. *Planned Parenthood v. Casey,* 1993.

27. See note 8 above.

28. For a well-researched and balanced presentation, listen to the audiotape "The Pill 101: the Abortifacient Action of Hormonal Contraceptives" by Dr. Chris Kahlenborn. To order from the Gift Foundation, see contact information in the Resources section.

29. Using figures of probability of conception and patterns of sexual activity, John Kippley has estimated that use of the IUD accounts for 247,800,000 "unknown" early abortions worldwide each year. The pill he estimates at 34,400,000 "unknown" early abortions worldwide each year (See *Birth Control & Christian Discipleship,* 2d ed. (Cincinnati, Ohio: Couple to Couple League, 1998), 14.

30. *Humanae Vitae,* n. 15.

31. If your own doctor is unable to help you in this regard, contact the Institute (see contact information in the Resources section).

32. See note 4 above.

33. *Gaudium,* n. 5.

34. In a survey by Dr. Josef Rotzer, out of fourteen hundred married couples using NFP,

there was not a single divorce among them (see DeMarco, 115).

35. Countless wives who use NFP in their marriages speak of the joy of being kissed without the suspicion that their husbands "want" something. This is the freedom and joy that NFP affords. It enables spouses to love each other for their own sake.

36. A source of encouragement for any wife hoping and praying for the conversion of her husband is the diary of Elisabeth Leseur entitled, *My Spirit Rejoices* (Manchester, NH: Sophia Institute Press, 1996). To order, see the Resources section.

37. The organization One More Soul has a national sterilization reversal hotline you can call for more information; see the Resources section.

38. There are several national NFP organizations listed in the Resources section of this book that offer classes throughout the country. Call your local diocesan offices or any of these organizations to find where classes are offered in your area. Taking a class is always recommended, but a home study course is also available through the Couple to Couple League (see the Resources section).

SEVEN
"I Do," But Not As God Intends

1. "The Love Within Families," 799.
2. *Time* Magazine, November 8, 1999, 66–69.
3. More than a few doctors have recognized the irony in the fact that they spend the first fifteen years of a woman's reproductive life helping her impede pregnancy and the second fifteen helping her conceive. Is it any wonder that a promiscuous culture bent on impeding pregnancy with high doses of fertility suppressant drugs and intrusive mechanical devices would experience a dramatic rise in rates of infertility when conception is desired?
4. Ironically, history's first test tube baby, Louise Brown, was born on July 25, 1978. This just so happened to be the tenth anniversary of the release of Pope Paul VI's encyclical *Humanae Vitae*, which upheld the intrinsic link between sex and procreation. Coincidence? Or is God making a subtle point? (Approximately one hundred thousand technologically produced children have been born in the United States alone since then.)
5. See Congregation for the Doctrine of the Faith, *Instruction on Respect for Human Life in Its Origin and on the Dignity of Procreation (Donum Vitae)*, n. 7. Hereafter referred to as *Donum*.
6. *Donum*, n. A1.
7. William E. May, *Marriage: The Rock on Which the Family is Built* (San Francisco: Ignatius, 1995), 98.
8. Spouses further violate their vows when they make recourse to the gametes of third parties (technically termed *heterologous fertilization*) or "use" the womb of

a surrogate mother for gestation, since the spouse's commitment to fidelity *"involves reciprocal respect of their right to become a father and a mother only through each other"* (*Donum*, n. A1).

9. *Donum*, n. B5.

10. See *Catechism*, n. 398.

11. *Humanae Vitae*, n. 16, emphasis added.

12. *Families*, n. 19.

13. See *Donum*, n. A1.

14. See *Donum*, n. B8.

15. Here again we see how the interior logic of contraception and technological repro-duction is related. Couples who engage in contracepted intercourse don't want God's will to be done in their sexual relationship but their own. Similarly, those who have recourse to technological fertilization aren't satisfied with God's will but seek their own. You might say we're dealing here with a "faucet approach" to fer-tility. Instead of trusting and respecting God's design, people demand the power to turn their fertility off when *they* want it off, and on when *they* want it on.

16. *Donum*, n. B8.

17. The following tragic story, told to me by a friend who teaches NFP, demonstrates how little some medical professionals know. After giving a presentation on how to interpret the signs of fertility, she noticed that a woman in the audience was beside herself with grief. It turned out she had been unable to conceive and for years had been following the advice of her doctor, who told her she could increase her chances if she waited to have intercourse until *after* her temperature shifted in her cycle. In actuality, the temperature shift indicates the *infertile* period of the cycle. Just prior to the temperature shift is the *most* fertile time.

18. See contact information for the Institute in the Resources section.

19. *Donum*, n. B8; quote within from *Familiaris*, n. 14.

20. *Denver Catholic Register*, July 21, 1999, 2.

21. If your own doctor can't supply a perforated condom, contact the Paul VI Institute (for contact information, see the Resources section).

EIGHT
When Saying "I Do" Is Impossible

1. Stanislaw Grygiel as quoted in, "The Church Must Guide the Sexual Revolution" (Zenit International News Agency, August 31, 1999), retrieved from www.ewtn.com/library/Theology/ZSEXREV.HTM.

2. Andrew Sullivan, *Virtually Normal*, cited in Philip F. Lawler's article "The Price of Virtue," *Catholic World Report*, July 1997, 59.

3. Nor does a brief chapter in this book. All I can do within the scope of this present project is address some of the questions and objections raised by predominantly

heterosexual audiences about homosexuality. For a more thorough treatment of the issue from a Catholic perspective, see John Harvey, *The Truth About Homosexuality* (San Francisco: Ignatius, 1996).

4. David Morrison, *Beyond Gay* (Huntington, Ind.: Our Sunday Visitor, 1999), 14.

5. See Congregation for the Doctrine of the Faith, *The Pastoral Care of Homosexuals*, n. 3. Hereafter referred to as *Pastoral.*

6. See *Pastoral*, 3.

7. When speaking of concupiscent desire for the opposite sex and for food and drink, it's necessary to use the adjective "disordered" because these desires aren't concupiscent in themselves. They're part of God's original plan, and when properly directed are very good. Homosexual desire, however, is disordered *in itself*. It wasn't part of God's original plan but is the result of original sin.

8. "Catholicism, Homosexuality, and Dignity," brochure published by Dignity, cited in *Beyond Gay*, p. 56.

9. See Ramesh Ponnuru, "Sexual Hangup," in *The National Review*, February 8, 1999, 42.

10. For those interested in a self-help approach to healing, I'd recommend Gerald Van den Aardweg, *The Battle for Normality: A Guide for (Self-) Therapy for Homosexuality* (San Francisco: Ignatius, 1997).

11. Mario Bergner, the man who gave these talks, has written a book that tells his story, called *Setting Love in Order* (Grand Rapids, Mich.: Baker, 1995). To order, see contact information in the Resources section.

12. It's beyond the scope of this book to debate different theories about the origins of homosexuality. There are several. My only point here is to explain briefly what made sense for me out of my own "identity crisis" and to note that these same insights have helped men with any and every degree of same-sex attraction better understand themselves.

13. Ask a homosexual man about his sexual fantasy life, and almost inevitably he'll describe himself uniting with idealized images of the masculine. This is simply the dynamic that I'm describing, as it happened in my own life, taken to its eroticized extreme. Leanne Payne, a counselor with years of experience helping homosexual men, describes this phenomenon as the "cannibal compulsion." Cannibals, apparently, typically eat only people they admire with the hopes of acquiring their traits. Homosexual men, she believes, seek to acquire that masculine part of themselves that they see in their sexual partner (or fantasized partner) but fear they lack in themselves. Her books *The Broken Image* (Grand Rapids, Mich.: Baker, 1981 and 1996) and *Healing Homosexuality* (Grand Rapids, Mich.: Baker, 1996) are well worth reading whether or not you struggle with same-sex attraction. To order from Baker Book House, see the Resources section.

14. St. Paul was tapping into a fundamental truth when he described the root of same-sex attraction as idolatry (see Rom 1:23-27).

15. Check the Resources section of this book for information on group programs of healing.

16. Look for contact information for both groups in the Resources section.

NINE
Saying "I Do" to God Alone

1. Revelation 21:1-3.
2. See *Body*, December 16, 1981.
3. *Body*, April 28, 1982.
4. *Body*, April 7, 1982. Manicheanism is an ancient dualistic heresy that views bodily things as evil, placing all emphasis on spiritual realities.
5. See *Body*, April 28, 1982.
6. John Paul II, *Letter to Women*, n. 3. I highly recommend this brief letter, as well as John Paul's more thorough treatment of the dignity and vocation of women in his Apostolic Letter *Mulieris Dignitatem* (hereafter referred to as *Mulieris*). To order both from the Daughters of St. Paul, see the contact information in the Resources section.
7. Grygiel.
8. *Mulieris*, n. 26.
9. *Mulieris*, n. 26.
10. Thanks to Mary Rousseau for this example. See her excellent article "Eucharist and Gender," *Catholic Dossier*, September/October 1996, 19–23, for a wonderful treatment of the issue of reserving priestly ordination to men.
11. See John Paul II, *Redemptor Hominis*, n. 1.

Resources

For Troubled Marriages

Gregory Popcak, MSW, LCWS
2416 Pennsylvania Ave.
Weirton, WV 26062
Counseling Hotline: 740-266-6461
gpopcak@exceptionalmarriages.com

Retrouvaille
This a very successful program designed to help heal troubled marriages
through frank and open dialogue.
1-800-470-2230
www.retrouvaille.org

Marriage Enrichment

Marriage Encounter
800-795-LOVE
www.wwme.org

Natural Family Planning

Billings Ovulation Method Association, USA
316 North 7th Ave.
St. Cloud, MN 56303
320-252-2100
www.boma-usa.com

Couple to Couple League
P.O. Box 111184
Cincinnati, OH 45211-1184
513-471-2000
www.ccli.org
ccli@ccli.org

Family of the Americas Foundation
P.O. Box 1170
Dunkirk, MD 20754
301-627-3346
www.familyplanning.net
familyplanning@yahoo.com

Northwest Family Services, Inc.
4805 N.E. Glisan St.
Portland, OR 97213
503-215-6377
www.nwfs.org
nfs@nwfs.org

Pope Paul VI Institute for the Study of Human Reproduction
6901 Mercy Rd.
Omaha, NE 68106
402-390-6600
www.popepaulvi.com

Educational Resources

Couple to Couple League
P.O. Box 111184
Cincinnati, OH 45211-1184
513-471-2000 (general info)
800-745-8252 (order line)
www.ccli.org
ccli@ccli.org

The Gift Foundation
P.O. Box 95
Carpentersville, IL 60110
800-421-GIFT
www.giftfoundation.org
info@giftfoundation.org

One More Soul
616 Five Oaks Ave.
Dayton, OH 45406
800-307-SOUL
www.omsoul.com
omsoul@omsoul.com

Real Love Productions (Mary Beth Bonacci)
P.O. Box 1324
Ft. Collins, CO 80522-1324
888-667-4992
www.reallove.net

Life After Sunday
Newsletter promoting John Paul II's vision of Catholic culture and the real
meaning of life.
P.O. Box 1761
Silver Spring, MD 20915
800-473-7980
www.lifeaftersunday.com

Homosexuality

Courage/EnCourage
210 W. 31st St.
New York, NY 10001
212-268-1010
NYCourage@aol.com
www.world.std.com/~courage

National Association for Research and Therapy of Homosexuality (NARTH)
16633 Ventura Blvd., Suite 1340
Encino, CA 91436
818-789-4440
narth@earthlink.net
www.narth.com

Personal Counseling/Referrals

Gregory Popcak, MSW, LCWS
2416 Pennsylvania Ave.
Weirton, WV 26062
Counseling Hotline: 740-266-6461
gpopcak@exceptionalmarriages.com

Saint Michael's Institute
286 Fifth Ave.
New York, NY 10001
212-629-4767
www.saintmichael.net
info@saintmichael.net

Sexual Addiction

Christian Alliance for Sexual Recovery
P.O. Box 2124
Tupelo, MS 38803-2124
662-844-5128
www.helpandhope.org

Sexaholics Anonymous (SA)
P.O. Box 111910
Nashville, TN 37222
615-331-6230
www.sa.org
saico@sa.org

Personal/Sexual Healing
(including homosexuality)

Redeemed Life Ministries
P.O. Box 1211
Wheaton, IL 60189-1211
630-668-0661
rlivesmin@aol.com

Pastoral Care Ministries
630-510-0487
charismc@aol.com
www.leannepaynenews.com

Desert Stream Ministries
P.O. Box 17635
Anaheim, CA 92817-7635
714-779-6899
info@desertstream.org
www.desertstream.org

Post-Abortion Healing

National Office of Post Abortion Reconciliation and Healing
P.O. Box 070477
Milwaukee, WI 53207-0477
800-5WE-CARE
www.marquette.edu/rachel
noparh@juno.com

Elliot Institute
P.O. Box 7348
Springfield, IL 62791-7348
www.afterabortion.org
dave12@famvid.com

Sterilization Reversal

One More Soul National Sterilization Reversal Hotline: 800-307-7685

Additional Resources by Christopher West

Naked Without Shame. Audiotape series on John Paul II's *Theology of the Body.* Contact *The Gift Foundation.* Call 800-421-GIFT.

Contact *Our Father's Will Communications* for a list of several other audio and video presentations by Christopher West. Call toll free 866-333-OFWC.

For access to various articles and other resources visit
www.theologyofthebody.com

Phone Numbers for Ordering Materials Recommended in This Text

Baker Book House: 616-957-3110
Catholic Answers: 888-291-8000
Catholics United for the Faith: 800-MY-FAITH
Couple to Couple League: 800-745-8252
Daughters of Saint Paul: 800-876-4463
The Gift Foundation: 800-421-GIFT
Ignatius Press: 800-651-1531
One More Soul: 800-307-SOUL
Our Sunday Visitor Press: 800-348-2440
Sophia Institute Press: 800-888-9344

Index